T5-AGV-190

BELMONT UNIVERSITY LIBRARY
BELMONT UNIVERSITY
1900 BELMONT BLVD.
NASHVILLE, TN 37212

the series on school reform

Patricia A. Wasley
Coalition of
Essential Schools

Ann Lieberman
NCREST

SERIES EDITORS

Joseph P. McDonald
Annenberg Institute
for School Reform

This series also incorporates earlier titles in the
Professional Development and Practice Series

CASE WRITERS

Dinah Brown
Philip Burke
Jonathan Cooper-Wiele
Jill Crawford
Tony Day
Julie Dunlap
Bruce Frana
Lisa Millenbah
Rhonda Niemi
Lynne Williams

CASE COMMENTATORS

Robert Allekotte
Cheryl Ashley
Jane Assmann
Debbie Baker
Don Daws
Anita Dupree
Eileen Dwell
Roy Ford
Jan Fulton
Shirley Gonsalves
Kay Gregory
Roger Harris
Linda Jewell
Susan Jones
Pat Kurtz
Terry Miller
Jo Ann Mosier
Paul Smith
Dana Tomlinson
Al Walters
Donn Weinholtz

RACING WITH THE CLOCK

MAKING TIME FOR
TEACHING AND LEARNING
IN SCHOOL REFORM

EDITED BY

Nancy E. Adelman
Karen Panton Walking Eagle
Andy Hargreaves

Teachers College, Columbia University
New York and London

Published by Teachers College Press, 1234 Amsterdam Avenue, New York, NY 10027

Copyright © 1997 by Teachers College, Columbia University

All rights reserved. No part of this publication may be reproduced or transmitted in any form or by any means, electronic or mechanical, including photocopy, or any information storage and retrieval system, without permission from the publisher.

The perspectives presented in this volume are derived from work conducted for the U.S. Department of Education, Office of Educational Research and Improvement, from 1991–1995 under Contract No. RR9112010. Any opinions, findings, conclusions, or recommendations expressed in this publication are those of the authors and editors and do not necessarily reflect the views of the U.S. Department of Education.

Library of Congress Cataloging-in-Publication Data

Racing with the clock : making time for teaching and learning in
  school reform / edited by Nancy E. Adelman, Karen Panton Walking
  Eagle, Andy Hargreaves.
      p.   cm. — (The series on school reform)
   Includes bibliographical references and index.
   ISBN 0-8077-3649-X (cloth : alk. paper). — ISBN 0-8077-3648-1
(pbk. : alk. paper)
   1. Teachers—Time management—United States—Case studies.
2. Teacher participation in administration—United States—Case
studies. 3. Educational change—United States—Case studies.
I. Adelman, Nancy E. (Nancy Elizabeth), 1944-   . II. Walking
Eagle, Karen Panton. III. Hargreaves, Andy. IV. Series.
LB2838.8.R33   1997
371.1'06—dc21   97-15313

ISBN 0-8077-3648-1 (paper)
ISBN 0-8077-3649-X (cloth)

Printed on acid-free paper
Manufactured in the United States of America

04 03 02 01 00 99 98 97   8 7 6 5 4 3 2 1

199497

BELMONT UNIVERSITY LIBRARY

LB
2838.8
.R33
1997

ABB-1510

Contents

Introduction

This is a volume of cases on the meaning and use of professional time in a school reform context. The writers are experienced teachers and other education professionals who are on the front lines of changing and improving our schools. Their stories form the core of the book: nine first-person accounts from teachers, with accompanying comments from colleagues, associates, and the editors of this volume about an experience that places extraordinary demands on time. The editors are research and evaluation specialists who observe and analyze what happens on the front lines during the educational change process. Their essays frame the cases—at the beginning of the book drawing a map of the issues to be raised and at the end summarizing the issues, possibilities, and unresolved questions. All of us—classroom practitioners and researchers alike—offer our stories and insights in the hope that they will be useful to others in provoking discussion about the relationship between teaching, time, and reform. We especially hope that they will be used by institutions that prepare new teachers and in venues where experienced teachers come together to replenish their professional commitment and enthusiasm.

OVERVIEW OF THE "MOTHER" STUDY

The cases in this volume emerged as one product of a larger study on the relationship between time and educational reform. Policy Studies Associates, Inc. (PSA), under contract with the U.S. Department of Education, recently completed a study of the uses of time in selected elementary and secondary schools around the country (Adelman, Haslam, & Pringle, 1996). The study's specific mandates were to examine the quantity and quality of students' uses of time in school and their uses of time during nonschool hours. Very early on in our work, however, we realized that we could not study the quantity and quality of educational time for students without simultaneously concerning ourselves with time as a critical factor in teachers' professional lives. Improved curriculum and instruction for students are, after all, direct by-products of the time available for teachers to consider and discuss, adopt and practice, and implement and refine different approaches to their work.

Our research design allowed us to observe and interview teachers in 14 sites, selected as examples of good practice on several dimensions related to the quantity and quality of time in school. The stories of educational change and reform in the teachers' voices that are at the core of this book represent a subgroup of the sites—all of them public schools serving a range of grade levels (although, at several of the schools, a graded school structure was increasingly irrelevant as faculty and administrators reconsidered the meaning of time during a student's total school career).

Although our initial hypotheses about the relationship between time and learning speculated that quantity of time would prove less important than quality, we nevertheless selected schools with both more and less instructional time than is typical in the United States. Thus, for example, one middle school had an extended school day on 4 days of the week, primarily to offer its inner-city students a "double dose" of language arts instruction. In contrast, faculty at a middle school in another city decided to sacrifice some instructional time to transportation in order to give students the community-based instructional experiences that were key to the school's overarching philosophy.

Our primary site-selection factors related to the quality of instructional time were multi-age student groupings (sometimes called an ungraded structure, particularly at the elementary school level) and flexible scheduling in middle and high schools. Multi-age groupings (e.g., classrooms housing 6-, 7-, and 8-year-olds) fundamentally alter the traditional patterns of American schooling, which are rooted in assumptions about uniformity in the time needed to learn. Similarly, in secondary schools, the dominance of the 45- to 50-minute class period has traditionally shaped the nature of curriculum delivery and instruction. Introducing flexibility into the schedule allows a qualitative reconceptualization of the available instructional time and how it might be used.

Although we were not able to spend extensive time at the schools in our sample, we learned a great deal about the effect of reform on teachers' lives during these brief visits. We talked with many perceptive practitioners who clearly had relected long and hard on the highs and lows, the give-and-take, and the pros and cons of ongoing reform efforts. Many of the schools that we visited had long ago institutionalized time-related reforms (e.g., site-based decision making, multi-age student grouping) that have only recently gained currency in the mainstream educational research and reform agendas. We were intrigued to discover that, despite their high comfort levels with and mastery of these kinds of reform strategies, faculty and other school staff in these places continued to refine their practice in ways that kept their professional lives dynamic, off-center, and often stressful. In other schools in our small sample, the time-related reforms were newer (although no school was less than 3 years into an overall school improvement plan). These places offered us windows on the early and middle stages of complex reform agendas. Here too we found practitioners who were analytical and self-conscious about their reform undertakings.

As long-time observers of the educational scene in the United States, we were struck by a distinctive difference in the climate of the current wave of school reform in comparison with earlier reform movements. The nature of many of the elements of reforms currently being implemented requires the active participation of teachers—and, therefore, their time. Further, the successful implementation of many of the reforms requires the willingness of teachers to undertake new roles and assume new responsibilities. Asking teachers to write thematic, interdisciplinary curriculum is change of quite a different order from adoption of a new textbook, even if it is a whole-language series. Similarly, having the authority to make final decisions about school schedules and how curriculum and instruction will be delivered is very different from serving on a committee that makes recommendations to a higher governing body. In schools where the improvement plan is truly systemic, teachers today are experiencing both empowerment and levels of stress that we need to understand more fully in order to help successful reforms expand and move forward. Almost always, we have found, the psychological highs and lows of the change process are somehow related to time.

Two key observations about teachers, time, and reform led to the development of this volume: (1) the articulateness of teachers in the schools that we visited about their commitment to and struggles with school reform and (2) our sense that the magnitude of the demands on teachers' time has escalated in reform contexts that are increasingly systemic and complex. The book is the product of our desire to capture school reform experiences (particularly as they are related to issues of time) in teachers' own words and to insert practitioners' voices into our own and the broader research and evaluation agenda for improving American education.

WHAT ARE CASES?

"Cases" are teaching and learning tools that have been used for years in graduate and professional schools, particularly in business, management, and public policy programs. In general, a case is a narrative describing in some detail a specific problem or issue encountered in the real world. A good case—in the sense that it is useful to others—is also an example or instance of something. For readers, it is evocative of experiences in their own careers or lives. A natural response to a good case is "Ah, this is a case of . . ."

because it stands for a class of issues or problems that are of concern to many people.

In the past decade or so, a growing network of professors, professional development experts, and technical assisters have begun to support, develop, and use a case literature in their work with both pre-service and experienced teachers. Lee Shulman (1986, 1987) has been a major proponent of cases prepared by practicing educators as a means to strengthening the knowledge base on teaching. Some of the centers of activity in developing and using cases for teacher preparation and professional development include WestEd (formerly the Far West Laboratory for Educational Research and Development) in San Francisco, Pace University in New York City, Virginia Polytechnic Institute in Blacksburg, and Michigan State University in Lansing (see also McAninch, 1993; Shulman, 1992; Wassermann, 1993, 1994). We suggest that readers of this volume who would like to connect with the growing network of educators who are using the case method in college and university classrooms or in school district professional development opportunities should begin their inquiries with these institutions. That is what we did before launching the project that led to this book.

As narratives, cases describe a situation in enough detail and with enough context to elicit reader reactions grounded in their own experiences and to stimulate debate about the causes of a situation, the actions that individuals took, or the ways in which a problem might be resolved. In a business school seminar, for example, a case might describe the negative impact of new personnel policies on employee morale and productivity. As individuals, in teams, or as a group, seminar members would develop possible approaches to resolving the problem. We can see this casebook on teachers, time, and reform that we have helped prepare used in this way in undergraduate and graduate teacher preparation programs. We can also imagine its use in less formal, continuous-improvement groups that form in schools that are undergoing change. We hope that it will also encourage the teachers who read it to challenge themselves and their colleagues to prepare cases of their own that can be the grist for ongoing staff discussions and debates around themes or topics of particular concern to them. Cases do not have to be bound into a book to be useful learning tools.

CREATING THE CASES IN THIS BOOK

Our idea of creating a casebook was formulated a short time after we had completed field work on our Uses of Time for Teaching and Learning study. Although that data-collection effort had focused primarily on the impacts of various time structures from the student perspective, as we have noted, teacher time issues arose consistently as a subtheme. Using our already-established relationships with teachers and principals in the public schools in the study (we had also prepared case studies of five private schools that either are residential or offer greatly extended school days to disadvantaged students), we invited teachers to participate who we thought would be interested in helping us probe more extensively into the relationship between time and their professional lives. Our intent was to assemble a group of teachers who were reflective and analytic and who could effectively represent and communicate about the time-related challenges that teachers and administrators in innovative schools have confronted. We urged principals to encourage and support the participation of the teachers selected, since their participation in our project would require a brief time away from the classroom.

Case Writers and Commentators

The group of four men and six women who accepted our invitation to help prepare this casebook are from schools in seven states. Two are no longer classroom teachers—one recently retired and the other became a school administrator. Three of the remaining teachers teach in the elementary grades; four teach social studies, mathematics, or English in the middle grades; and one is a high school science teacher. The length of their teaching experience spans a period of less than 5 years to more than 20 years. The largest number have taught between 5 and 10 years.

The individuals who prepared the commentaries that accompany each case were selected by the teacher-writers themselves. They represent a range of people with knowledge of and a vested interest in a given school and its reform efforts. These individuals included, for example, principals, department chairpersons, other teachers, parents, and college faculty. These voices offer different perspectives and interpretations of the particular situations described by the teachers and raise further questions and topics for discussion. In addition, for each case we—the editors—prepared an introductory profile of the school and an analysis of the issues involved.

Although the names and titles of all case writers and commentators are listed at the beginning of the volume, we and they decided together that a particular name would not be directly associated with a specific case or commentary. The purpose of this strategy was to allow more freedom to raise difficult or contentious issues in the cases. Perhaps this was unnecessary, but we did not wish to cause the teachers any political problems at their home schools. In addition, school names are fictitious.

Preparing the Cases

After the teachers accepted our invitation to be involved in the project, we asked them to begin reflecting on their work experiences and to focus on a problem or dilemma related to teacher time that they have encountered as their schools have engaged with change and reform. They were given the option of focusing on a specific incident or problem that illustrates the effect of the innovation on their use of time, or they could discuss their experiences in more general terms (e.g., a description of the modifications and adaptations that have unfolded over the course of the reform's implementation). In addition, each teacher received a packet of materials with examples of cases, as well as background information on how and why cases are used in teacher education.

All participants attended a two-day weekend workshop at our offices in Washington, D.C., in November 1994 (with the expenses covered by our project, including the cost of a substitute teacher for one day). This workshop was facilitated by project staff and by Andy Hargreaves of the Ontario Institute for Studies in Education as consultant to the project. Hargreaves, a contributing editor to this casebook, has studied and written extensively on the topics of time, teachers' work, and educational change. His insights appear in Chapter 5, summarizing the issues that the teachers write about in the body of the text and suggesting areas for future thought and action.

On the first day of the workshop, the teachers worked together in small and large groups, discussing and reflecting on examples of educational change that they had experienced or were currently experiencing, and the impact the changes had on their work. Hargreaves, along with PSA staff, encouraged the participants to discuss concrete examples and their meaning with the rest of the group. Any points about time, work, and change were gathered together on flip-chart paper as a reference point for future dialogue and writing. The first day ended with a discussion and analysis of the content and structure of cases during which the teachers focused on the characteristics of well-constructed cases.

The second day was devoted to developing preliminary drafts of the cases. Most of the teachers in the group worked alone, although two teachers who team teach at the same school decided to write a single case. Audiotape and computer facilities were available for those who wished to use them, as well as quiet offices for contemplation. Once initial drafts had been developed, teachers worked in pairs, threes, or fours, sharing their drafts and giving feedback on them, emphasizing what they liked in style and substance about the drafts and also what they found underdeveloped or problematic. At the end of two days, the teachers returned home with drafts of their cases in various stages of completeness.

Over the next few months, the teachers worked closely with PSA staff—via telephone and correspondence—to expand and revise their cases through further dialogue about the issues, perspectives, and conclusions they wished to convey. When they were comfortable with their drafts, they shared them with the individuals whom they had selected to be commentators. PSA staff also worked directly with the commentators as they prepared and revised their pieces.

The whole process of developing the casebook took about 6 months. It could be done more quickly under other circumstances—if, for example, the writers all lived and worked in the same area and could meet on a regular basis.

The teachers who contributed their time, thoughts, and energy to the creation of this volume did so with a great deal of interest and enthusiasm. Each was eager to share experiences and frustrations, and to learn how peers in other innovative settings were coping with the time pressures that seem to naturally accompany efforts to introduce and successfully implement educational change and reform. However, according to these teacher-writers, the most important benefit of participating in this project was that their opinions, analyses, and feelings were sought, acknowledged, and valued—in their view, a rare and unusual experience for most classroom teachers. Specifically, they described how being invited to Washington for an all-expenses-paid-weekend to think about and reflect on their work made them "feel like professionals." In addition, receiving financial compensation for their finished product (they were paid a stipend when the final draft was complete), and being listed as case writers, contributed to positive feelings about their professional worth.

We find these reflections about the event that we sponsored to be very poignant comments on the status of teaching in America. The apparent novelty of the experience and the teachers' appreciative reaction to it highlight one of the underlying problems that hinder the efforts to successfully reform and improve education: We do not listen to all the voices that could help refine the change process and make it less perilous. Based on the cases in this book, it is clear that teachers have much to say about their experiences with time and reform.

Karen Panton Walking Eagle

CHAPTER 1

Framing the Cases: Time for Change

Nancy E. Adelman

The 10 teachers who prepared the nine cases that are at the heart of this volume work in schools and school districts that have undertaken substantial reform efforts during the 1990s. As the Introduction noted, the contexts for these efforts vary greatly, as do the individual reform strategies adopted. However, in each instance, the nature of the planned reforms and the process of implementing them have had profound implications for teachers' professional roles, responsibilities, and time. Indeed, based on our continuing exploration of the uses of time for teaching and learning, we are prepared to assert that any hope of systemic improvement of education in the United States is inextricably linked to the generosity with which teachers contribute the resource over which they have the most control—their time. In this chapter, we frame some key issues governing the interrelationships among teacher professionalism, time, and school reform that the cases illustrate in more concrete terms.

We have found that certain kinds of issues are associated with different stages of the change or reform process. Early on, there is a planning stage, which can be shorter or longer in duration depending on the wisdom of change leaders. The experiences of teachers during this period are critically important to the coherence and integrity of a reform effort. In the middle stage, reforms are actually being introduced and institutionalized into the daily fabric of life in schools and classrooms. Frequently, it is at this middle stage that reform agendas founder, as forward momentum dwindles and initiatives peter out. Sometimes, however, full implementation does occur. Then, the change process moves into another stage requiring time for reflection, assessment, and reevaluation of priorities to ensure continuous progress. The nine cases in this book fall rather neatly into these three stages, which serve as the organizers for the remainder of this chapter and for grouping the cases into the chapters that follow.

1

THE PLANNING STAGE

Roland Barth (1990) has observed a misguided tendency among educators—teachers included—to view schools "as places where children learn and adults teach" (p. 50). It is true that the ultimate goal of reform is (or should be) improved student learning and that the centrality of this goal too often becomes lost in the reform process (Fullan, 1991; Weiss, Cambone, & Wyeth, 1992). However, in the context of the comprehensive strategies that have characterized the "second wave" reforms of the 1990s (e.g., systemic reform, restructuring, reculturing), teachers have been asked to assume new responsibilities and adopt new practices that are substantially different from traditional notions about what it means to be a teacher. Under these circumstances, teachers need time to be learners themselves—a truth that is rarely factored into reform schedules and is quite likely an important variable in the dismal track record of educational change efforts over the past 30 years.

Several cases in this book richly illustrate the problem of finding or making time for teachers to examine, accept, and experiment with proposed reforms. In "Change: Making It Work," for example, the author describes a situation in which the district leadership imposed comprehensive, top-down reform with an expectation of instant implementation. She notes that "[t]here was little time for in-depth staff development, and no time for reflection or for priorities to be established." Needless to say, the result was consternation and resistance among teachers. There is, however, a saving grace in this district for some teachers: an enrichment program for students offered during vacation periods where teachers are encouraged to learn and experiment with new materials and instructional practices. The author of this case is now the administrator of the enrichment program. An astute observer of the roadblocks to change that occurred when she was in the classroom, she has internalized what she learned into her leadership style and the rules that govern her program, creating a learning laboratory for teachers in her district. Thus, some good has come out of a misguided approach to districtwide reform.

If comprehensive districtwide school reform is difficult to achieve by mandate and without adequate accommodation of the learning curves of individual teachers, imagine the challenges inherent in the reform of an entire state education system. In "Portfolio Prison—Escape or Parole," we hear from a teacher who was thrown head-first into her state's new system of school and teacher accountability—portfolio assessments of students at selected grade levels. While her state must be given some credit for trying to supply adequate technical assistance and for not immediately applying the rewards and sanctions aspects of its new education legislation, the stress and upheaval that learning-on-the-fly produce for teachers are readily apparent in her story.

She and most of her colleagues were asked to help students develop port-folios without ever having seen one. No wonder her account of her first year under this new system uses words like *angry*, *resentful*, and *anxiety*. Several years later, she is undefeated but hardly unscathed—still learning how to fit portfolio development into the academic year without losing time for instruction and still not wholly committed to portfolio assessment as an appropriate statewide school accountability mechanism.

"Change: Making It Work" and "Portfolio Prison—Escape or Parole" are cases of mandated educational change where policymaking and planning took place at the district and state levels respectively with little or no teacher input and, therefore, little or no initial ownership or understanding of the value of specific reform strategies at the school and classroom levels. In "From Dedication to Despair," we have a different situation—the creation of a new, innovative school—but the same lack of attention to time for planning and practice. This time, teachers are in control and believe in the reform principles on which the school is founded, but they have been naive about the time requirements of an undertaking such as theirs. They actually waivered their contractual planning time and simultaneously committed themselves to developing an entire middle-school curriculum from scratch, during the school year and with students present. The title of this case may sound hyperbolic, but, as you will see, it is not. The author is just plain exhausted.

Time for planning and exploration and risk-free time for practicing new classroom strategies and behaviors seem like obvious stages of the educational change process. Yet, as these three cases demonstrate, these phases of reform are often omitted for reasons of time, money, or sheer thoughtlessness. Not many of us would agree to get up on a stage in public and perform without plenty of opportunity to practice the act. Why, then, should teachers agree to perform new parts without benefit of rehearsals? Under such conditions, it is little wonder that a common response to calls for educational change is to close the classroom door.

THE IMPLEMENTATION STAGE

Generally speaking, the implementation stage of educational reform occurs after a few risk-taking teachers have piloted new materials, new instructional strategies, new governance structures, new organizational arrangements, and so on. If the results have been positive or at least neutral, a decision is made to expand the initiative—in the current language of systemic reform, to "scale up." Now, there is an expectation that everyone will come aboard and that those who led the way will assist their peers in learning the new practices and behaviors.

This stage of the change process has its own pitfalls. It is, in particular, a time when the pioneers can become overextended and frustrated and when the resisters dig in their heels. Frequently, this stage ends with the original enthusiasts' institutionalizing the parts of the innovation that they value in their own classrooms or teaching teams, but with little or marginal impact on the organization as a whole. The status remains quo.

Educational innovations in America seem to spread like kudzu. At the time that we were visiting schools and meeting the teachers who prepared the cases in this volume, the innovation du jour was teacher-developed, thematic, interdisciplinary curriculum. (The study team suspected that the source of this movement was the Carnegie Council on Adolescent Development's influential 1989 report *Turning Points*.) The expectation that teachers would write and implement their own curriculum was everywhere and, for the most part, teachers were enthusiastic about wearing this new hat. However, it led to some very problematic situations in terms of demands on professional time.

In "Teacher-as-Juggler," a middle-school teacher talks about being "a master of curriculum evolution," a skill that he has developed in the context of establishing a community-based, student-centered alternative middle school with an emphasis on experiential learning. He laments, however, that "I can do anything, but I cannot do everything." Because so far he and his colleagues barely stay one day ahead of the students with their curriculum development, this teacher has not been able to find time to learn new instructional strategies. In the classroom, his students receive their innovative, thematic, interdisciplinary curriculum through stand-and-deliver methods. From the students' perspective, this must not seem very "alternative."

The author of "Reclaiming Reform" is also committed to the ubiquitous teacher-developed, thematic, interdisciplinary curriculum, which is one of the planks in his school's improvement platform. He has had a hard time, however, focusing his colleagues' attention on this aspect of the grand design, in all likelihood because curriculum development is a lot harder and more time-consuming than some other reform elements that have been fully implemented, with gratifying results in terms of student outcomes. Professional planning time when curriculum development might occur is less of a problem in this school than in the juggler's. However, the issue seems to be whether the majority of teachers see a payoff in learning the role of curriculum developer. Given that the school has turned itself around without implementing this particular reform, perhaps it is just one innovation too many.

Curriculum development also occupied many on- and off-clock hours for the teaching team who prepared "Dual-Language Dilemma." In a school that has made many changes to improve education and services for its largely working-class, Hispanic student population, these two teachers were among the most energetic reformers. They voluntarily developed, piloted, and demonstrated the effectiveness of a two-way bilingual (Spanish-English, English-Spanish) classroom for both the Hispanic and Anglo students that they shared. Their dilemma is that they cannot get colleagues to replicate their experiment. Implementation of curriculum reform is therefore at a standstill and for a whole host of reasons detailed in their case and the commentaries that accompany it, expansion of this innovation seems improbable. As I noted earlier, this is a common result during the implementation stage in the change process: The planned change is ultimately confined to a few classrooms.

Professional development is nearly always the strategy of choice when reformers are ready to extend implementation of innovations to include larger numbers of classrooms. We know a lot more than we used to about what constitutes high-quality professional development, but that is not by any means what is actually delivered to teachers. Perhaps that is why the case entitled "Classroom Teaching and Professional Development: Must I Choose?" seems such a refreshing example of professional growth in a state, district, and school reform environment that is more supportive than most. It is also a fine illustration of the time dilemmas that arise for talented classroom teachers when leadership opportunities tempt them to take on multiple roles. The change and improvement process intellectually awakens many teachers, as it did this one. Sometimes, the result is that good teachers find a new career path with seemingly higher prestige and leave the classroom. However, the author of this case has taken stock and decided that being a classroom teacher is her primary role; her other professional responsibilities simply enrich what she brings to her students.

In contrast to the cases introduced as examples of the planning and practice stage of reforms, the cases illustrating the implementation stage are mainly situations where control of the change process is at the school level. The pressures and tensions of implementation that these teachers and their colleagues feel are, therefore, self-imposed, and in some ways, this takes a greater psychological toll when implementation problems arise. There is no "them" to blame or rail at. There is only "us." In a number of the cases, you will find the authors speaking of very personal feelings: guilt, letting colleagues down, fear of being thought a quitter. This is precisely why the idea of continuous school improvement is such an important ingredient in a successful, sustained school reform process. Not every planned change will work in a given context, but if there is provision for monitoring the implementation process and revisiting the best-laid plans, problems do not become immovable barriers against progress. This brings us to the introduction of the remaining two cases in this book.

THE CONTINUOUS IMPROVEMENT STAGE

The research literature on school change is replete with examples of failure. Seymour Sarason (1971, 1990, 1996) continues to believe that the more things change, the more they stay the same—or get worse. However, there are examples of schools that have fully implemented their original reform vision, including strategies that allow for much more flexibility in the use of teachers' professional time. We visited two of them. Over more than 20 years, staff in both of these schools have continued to refine and adapt their programs, constantly questioning the appropriateness and quality of the education that they offer the populations they serve. Their success with students is well documented. Yet the cases that you will read are not happy stories. The success of their strategies has become a two-edged sword.

"Quality Time in an Alternative School" is an ironic tale of policy catching up with innovative practice and restraining it. For years, this school made its own decisions about the use of time, curriculum and instruction, student assessment, and governance. The back-to-basics movement caused it a slight setback at one point, but, in general, the school was allowed to march to its own drummer. In the early 1990s, however, site-based decision making was "discovered" by policymakers in this district. It became mandated and regulated in ways that harshly curtailed the control that staff had always had— particularly over the use of time. For the author of this case, a founding father of the innovative program, it was too much. He retired to regain control over his time, much of which he still dedicates to the school.

In "The Erosion of Site-Based, Shared Decision Making," the culprit is reputation, not policy. In its more than 20 years of serving square-peg and highly at-risk high school students, what was originally a tiny alternative program has grown into a real school serving hundreds of students. Obviously, the need for the flexibility that the school offers (including flexibilities in time for both teachers and students) has increased. In addition, the school has worked for a lot of young people who can today hang their high school diplomas rather than their heads. For the teacher who prepared the case, however, something has been lost in the translation from small to medium-large. He believes that it is the trivializing of what used to be real staff empowerment in the decision-making process.

What both of these cases of mature reform illustrate is the fragility of the change process and its vulnerability to the passage of time as well as shortages of time. Time never stands still, and circumstances inevitably change, as do people. The perceptions of these two teachers, comparing the way it was with the way it is, are their truths. But what are the perceptions of teachers who have worked in these schools for 5 years rather than 25? We do not know, but we do know from our own observations that the spirit of continuous progress lives in both schools and that staff will probably find ways to turn the issues they currently face to good advantage.

TRANSITION TO THE TEACHER'S VOICE

You are now about to leave behind the voices of researchers and move into the world of teachers reflecting on their professional lives in schools that are trying to design, implement, and sustain changes that produce positive student outcomes. Each case represents a different set of constraints on and supports for reform. All of them represent situations in which teachers have given freely of their time to try to make the education system better.

If you use the cases for professional development purposes, assign someone to keep a running tally of the mentions of *time* in the discussion as participants comment on and personalize the experiences of the authors. I guarantee that use of the term will be nearly unconscious and the context very often clichéd: make the most of our time, timely ideas, just in time, and so forth. We attuned ourselves to mentions of time for 4 years, and it was astonishing how often time was the culprit when something had not worked. It was also astonishing how invisible time and its structures were until there was impetus for some kind of major adjustment in the workplace. Then, there was a concerted effort to find time, make time, or cut time in half.

This volume ends with a summary essay by Andy Hargreaves, a longtime observer of teachers, time, and reform. His insights and proddings to focus attention on restructuring educational time provide a valuable capstone essay to this volume. Today, he makes a half-joke when he says that he has moved on to space, for time and space are intimately related. Our own continuing work on teachers, time, and reform finds a strong relationship between teachers' perceptions of time for instruction and the size of their classes, for example. Time seems far more pressed when there is a crowd than when there is a reasonable space around each person in a classroom.

When you begin to analyze people's perceptions of the conditions under which they work, the discussion can very quickly take a philosophical turn that delves deep. We hope that the cases in this volume will be useful for stimulating both nitty-gritty, practical discussions of restructuring time to support school change and more intense debates of the relationship between time and structural reforms of the larger educational system.

CHAPTER 2

The Planning Stage: The Need for Time to Explore and Learn

The three cases in this chapter illustrate some of the problems that can arise when, in the rush to implement bold new ideas, educational reformers underestimate the time necessary for classroom practitioners to understand and come to terms with what is being asked of them. This miscalculation is often self-defeating because it can actually impede the pace of change by diverting teachers' time and energy away from a rational examination of the proposed new practices and toward an enervating and unproductive period of complaints, resistance, and recrimination. As you consider the situations described by these teachers, think about alternative strategies that might have been employed to eliminate some of the inevitable frustrations associated with the process of change and innovation.

CHANGE: MAKING IT WORK

School District Profile: Southport Elementary School District

The Southport Elementary School District is a relatively small K–6 school district in the Southwest. Over half of the district's students are Hispanic, many with limited English proficiency. Per capita income in the area served is about $6,600, and the families of about 60% of enrolled students live below the poverty level. The average student transiency rate for the district is 42%. Despite the district's demographic profile, its students are educationally successful. For example, sixth-graders recently scored in the 97th percentile in mathematics on the state's test of basic skills.

This district's 12 schools operate on a year-round schedule, partly to accommodate a rapidly growing student population, but partly because of a belief that students and teachers alike are better served by spacing vacation periods throughout the year. Year-round scheduling was first introduced in two schools in 1974 during one population growth spurt. By 1980, enrollment pressures had eased, but staff and parents at the two schools convinced the school board to retain the year-round schedule. When enrollments again began to escalate in the 1980s, the district introduced year-round schedules in all of the schools.

In addition to expanding year-round scheduling to all schools, administrators in this district imposed a top-down, comprehensive reform plan. Implementation of the plan has led to a good deal of tension between the district administration and the teachers' union. Building principals have been required to conduct most in-service sessions, whether they are expert in a particular aspect of reform or not. Teams of central office administrators visit schools regularly to evaluate progress and provide feedback to principals on progress in implementing the mandated reforms.

Case: Elementary School Teacher/Administrator

My elementary school district of approximately 10,000 students is located along the Mexican border in California. Forty percent of the student population is limited-English-proficient, and more than 60% of all students live in households where the annual income is below the poverty level. One of the many ways we strive to meet the instructional needs of this diverse population is to have all 12 of the schools in the district operate on a year-round calendar.

Eight of the schools are four-track schools, which means the students and teachers are assigned to either the A, B, C, or D track. Each track has a different calendar and vacation schedule. At any given time, students and teachers in three of the tracks are in school and those in the fourth track are on vacation or "intersession." When those in the fourth track return, another track goes on intersession. Under this system, each track rotates through a cycle in which they are "three months on, one month off." Each track has three intersession breaks during the school year. The remaining four schools in the district are on a single-track calendar, which means all of the students and staff in each school follow the same calendar and are on intersession break at the same time. However, each of these four schools is on a different track (A, B, C, or D). Their calendars match the corresponding A, B, C, and D track schedule that operates within each of the eight four-track schools in the district.

The Extended Year School (EYS) is a voluntary 15-day program that operates during each intersession. It is designed to increase the number of instructional days available for students. "Off-track" students (i.e., those on vacation) from throughout the district are transported to a single-track school whose students are also on vacation. An average of 500 students attending each session use all of the school's classrooms. By participating in EYS, students can attend school for up to an additional 30 days per year, increasing their total instructional days up to 215 each year. In addition, teachers who

work at EYS during their intersession earn significant additional pay. Originally implemented to meet the needs of low-achieving students, this innovative program has proven to be a key factor in implementing change throughout the district.

During the first 5 years of my teaching career, my district went through
many dramatic and rapid changes. Our district superintendent was a strong
leader with a well-articulated educational vision. New programs, new policies, and new expectations for teachers were introduced in quick succes-
sion, and teachers were expected to implement several new programs and
teaching methods within a very short period. The following areas were affected by these changes:

- *Technology.* Each classroom is now equipped with three computers,
and students are required to work on the computer for at least 20 minutes
per day, using a program related to classroom learning.
- *Instruction.* Teachers are expected to provide instruction using several new strategies, including cooperative learning, heterogeneous grouping, and open-ended questioning. Strategies that help to develop critical
thinking skills are also required.
- *Curriculum.* There is an emphasis on thematic, integrated, literature-
based language arts, social studies, science, and mathematics instruction.
- *Record-keeping and accountability.* A new accountability system,
which requires extensive record-keeping and documentation on each student, was introduced. In addition, teachers' workloads increased when the
district introduced the new Skills for Students' Success program, which is
designed to increase homework completion rates and improve communication between home and school. Under the new system, teachers prepare
written daily school reports, and they must monitor whether parents have
checked and signed their children's homework. The district has also given
parents a written "guarantee" that all students will be reading at grade level
by the end of the second grade.
- *Testing.* An intensive test-preparation program was introduced and
increased pressure was placed on teachers to ensure that students' test scores
improved.

Few teachers would argue that any of these changes have been unnecessary or detrimental to students; however, the majority of teachers were
overwhelmed by the magnitude of the changes and by the pace at which
they were expected to be implemented. Teachers barely had time to become familiar with one new program before the next one "came down the
pike." They also felt that they were given little or no opportunity to participate in the decision-making or design process for any of the new programs.

This sentiment increased their feelings of frustration and overshadowed their willingness to accept the changes. Although district administrators provided as much support as they could, they too were under tremendous pressure to monitor, evaluate, and demonstrate increased student achievement. There was little time for in-depth staff development, and no time for reflection or for priorities to be established.

As the quantity of new programs increased, the quality of the implementation process for each program decreased. Even high-achieving, "go-getter" teachers were stretched to the limit and felt helpless, overburdened, and unappreciated. Although our district had attracted national attention because of these innovations and because of our students' impressive achievement scores, there was no great feeling of pride among teachers. Instead, morale was at an all-time low, and union grievances were at an all-time high.

During this period of change, I made the transition from classroom teacher to school administrator. Because of my personal experiences with the change process, I had learned a great deal about the extent to which it can affect classroom teaching and learning. As a result, my goal during training was to learn all I could, as an instructional leader, about influencing change. I wanted to become an administrator who was a change agent for education, one who could introduce changes that would have positive, long-term effects on instruction. As I studied more about the dynamics of change and analyzed the leadership style of my superintendent, I realized that although I was impressed by the extent of the changes that had occurred in the district, I was disappointed in the way in which they had been implemented.

After my promotion to administrator of EYS, the superintendent who had been responsible for the major changes in the district retired, and someone with a very different leadership style and agenda for change became superintendent. The change in district leadership enabled me to further examine and reflect on the relationship between leadership style and organizational change. In fact, many of my beliefs about the change process are a direct result of my experiences with, and observations of, the past and current superintendents.

I believe that change is healthy and that significant changes do need to take place in education. However, more important, I believe people need time to accept and adapt to change, and to practice any new skills that are required. Only then can change truly be institutionalized. We would never expect a student to be able to multiply a two-digit number by another two-digit number without first teaching him or her the necessary skills *and* providing ample time to practice. So why would we expect a teacher to be able to successfully manage a cooperative learning group without the same opportunities to learn and practice the skills that are needed?

"Practice" by definition involves an element of "freedom from risk." It is a time for seeking and receiving constructive feedback—from oneself or others—and for monitoring and adjusting one's performance without worrying about being judged or evaluated. It is difficult for teachers (especially those who are averse to taking risks) to find either the time or the "freedom" to experiment with and practice new teaching techniques and strategies. I know many teachers are reluctant to try new strategies because they fear the principal will enter the classroom, without warning, and find them in the middle of an instructional experiment that is not working. With less than 2 years to demonstrate their competence in order to make tenure, new teachers often feel obligated to "be perfect" at all times. What better way to avoid "mistakes" than to not take chances?

As the administrator for EYS, I have been able to practice my beliefs about implementing change. EYS serves as a fertile "practice ground" for the teachers who participate, and I view one of my primary responsibilities as facilitating and supporting these teachers' professional development. Because they are not evaluated while they are working here, EYS provides a risk-free environment in which teachers can grow, explore, and experiment. In addition, because they are working at a different school and with a different class, the teachers experience an even greater sense of freedom to experiment.

Although our new superintendent has made significant progress in establishing a new "culture" in our district, teachers are still wary of change. One way we at EYS have dealt with this resistance is to pilot new curricular ideas and instructional strategies before they are implemented districtwide. Because EYS teachers represent all the schools in the district, they can bring back firsthand information about what was, or was not, successful in their EYS classroom to staff at their regular school. This strategy helps to validate the change process and ensures that an experienced resource—the EYS teacher—is present in each school.

Feedback from EYS teachers has been overwhelmingly positive. Instead of feeling "burned out" by working through their intersession break, teachers report that they are invigorated, and they return to their schools inspired with new ideas and teaching strategies. New teachers especially gain confidence and expertise because they have had the opportunity to practice in a supportive and nonthreatening atmosphere.

Participation in EYS is voluntary. Unfortunately, this means that the teachers who are most in need of "practice" are not always the ones who elect to teach during their intersession. Another source of frustration is the limited time available. EYS sessions are only 15 days long, with one day reserved for in-service training and classroom preparation. In addition, EYS is a very expensive discretionary program and is frequently "under the gun" for budget cuts. As a result of the most recent cuts, daily instruction time has been reduced from 6 to 4 hours.

Even with these limitations, however, EYS has met its goal of providing students with additional instruction to support achievement. An added benefit is that it has also been a valuable resource to teachers involved in the process of continual improvement.

Commentary: Teacher

I have been an elementary school teacher in this district for the past 6 years. During this time, I have taught fourth- and fifth-grade students at the Extended Year School on three occasions. EYS has proven to be extremely popular among teachers who have taught here. In fact, many of us have been "repeat customers," having taught during more than one intersession.

In the years that I have worked in this district, many new programs have been implemented. Unfortunately, in many cases teachers were not adequately prepared or trained for the changes that were introduced. Although teachers—or people in general—idealistically embrace the idea of change as a means of achieving improvements, in reality they tend to shy away from implementing the changes that are required, because of fear. Thus, the unending stream of new programs and policies that were introduced in this district—and the resulting need for ongoing change—led to a great deal of fear and resentment among teachers in the district.

EYS was among the many new programs that were introduced. It was not met with resentment, however, because it is a voluntary program. The benefits of teaching at EYS include (1) true autonomy in the classroom; (2) a supportive administrator who is willing to drop everything to offer assistance; (3) a forum in which to put new district programs into practice; and (4) the opportunity to teach a choice of interesting and innovative curricula—including cutting-edge math replacement units.

Unfortunately, because EYS is a voluntary program, it is difficult to involve a wide range of teachers. One reason is that EYS occurs at the end of each track period—a time when the last thing most teachers want to do is work. They are typically tired and ready for free time. Currently, only those who are self-motivated to improve their teaching, and those who need an additional paycheck, apply to work at EYS. I believe that unless incentives are introduced, the number of teachers who decide to teach in EYS will continue to be limited, and only a small cross-section of teachers will realize the benefits of the program.

The most obvious incentive would be to increase the EYS salary. Because this is unlikely, another possibility would be for the district to recognize time spent teaching in EYS as contributing toward professional growth and development. Thus, the more sessions taught, the higher up one would move on the salary scale. If budgetary concerns make these two options unlikely, another less costly incentive would be for the state of California to recognize time spent working at EYS as professional growth hours and to allow this work experience to satisfy certain state credential renewal requirements.

EYS provides a new and unique teaching experience for those who choose to participate. However, therein lies the rub: Only those individuals who have the energy and motivation, and who are willing to try new experiences—to risk feeling some discomfort as they experiment with new teaching strategies—are going to benefit from the opportunities EYS provides. Without additional incentives, the challenge will remain: How can we get more teachers to want to be involved in EYS so that they can practice and enhance their teaching skills and learn to view change more positively and accept it more easily?

Commentary: District Administrator

Because our school district has many of the demographic features commonly associated with poor academic performance, the former superintendent sought to introduce changes that would have a positive impact on the academic performance of the large number of at-risk students in our schools. As this case points out, his arrival also served to highlight two important issues: (1) the importance of timing in implementing change, and (2) the strategies for ensuring that teachers accept and implement reforms.

The teachers' union was opposed to the former superintendent even before he arrived. He had been hired to bring change to the district, and the speed with which he introduced change led to a barrage of questions and complaints by teachers. Although it is true that the superintendent could have engaged in more collaborative decision-making and design processes, it is questionable whether any of the new, powerful programs would have come to fruition had he taken this approach. "Hell no, we won't go" was the prevalent feeling among many teachers. Their uncooperative attitude, it seems, would have obstructed change efforts and, ultimately, would have had an extremely negative impact on the achievement of some students.

Those seeking to implement change must acknowledge that all individuals (including teachers) learn at different rates. In the case of a school district, the process should accommodate among individual teachers the range of differences in their ability to adapt to new teaching methods and classroom routines. Nevertheless, in my opinion, the superintendent's ultimate goal of achieving improvements in student achievement should not have been negotiable and not held hostage by individual teachers who were unwilling or unable to make the changes necessary under the circumstances. We owe that much to our students and to the parents who drop off their most prized possessions at school every morning.

The second issue that is raised in the case is the critical role that the Extended Year School—which was unilaterally established by the former superintendent—can play in helping teachers to learn, grow, and become more comfortable with change. EYS is a wonderful "practice ground" for the teachers and students who attend during their vacation time. Although it is a "risk-free" environment, teachers are expected to teach new curriculum and to use proven instructional strategies that they might not normally use in their regular classrooms. However, EYS's long-term impact on teachers' professional growth cannot be assumed or taken for granted; it depends on teachers' transferring their newly acquired skills and knowledge from the artificial EYS setting of only 15 days to their regular classrooms. In addition, improvement depends on the continued commitment of teachers and on the focused support of school administrators, who should offer constructive feedback to teachers on a regular basis and who must willingly assume the role of instructional guides to encourage teachers to stretch and grow.

Analysis: Editor

In this case, the author—a teacher who has recently moved into administration—describes the key characteristics of her district and the reform plan that it has been implementing for a number of years. As a participant-observer in the change process, she has drawn her own conclusions about how change does and does not happen in schools. Her perceptions validate and verify important elements of a theory of educational change that has been evolving over a 25–30 year period.

As is so often the situation at both district and school levels, this story begins with a leader hired with a specific mandate to bring about change. In short order, his plan emerged and was imposed in a top-down manner. The global nature of the plan gives the impression that the education situation in this district was dire, when in fact it seems that students were achieving quite well. In other words, the need for change of the magnitude proposed was simply not perceived by district veterans. This superintendent violated one of the basic lessons that we have learned about the change process: the need for a shared vision that all parties believe in. As Michael Fullan reminds us in *Change Forces* (1993), building consensus around a shared vision takes time. A bad start can make change take even longer.

The individual elements of the superintendent's reform plan that are listed in the case tell an interesting story of their own. Most of the buzz words of the 1990s are present: integrated, thematic curriculum; cooperative learning; and so on. These strategies are generally adopted in the belief that they will support more active, constructivist, and probably noisier learning environments. Perhaps the superintendent understood this. However, other elements of the plan—daily reporting, specified minutes per day on the computer, test preparation—tend in the opposite direction, toward greater rationalization and bureaucratic control of the education process. Creating interdisciplinary curriculum and learning to use new instructional strategies is a nonlinear reform requiring a lot of professional development time. Preparing daily reports to parents (the kind of reform that quickly becomes *pro forma*) and scheduling students on the computer also take time, but they are far easier to implement—however resentfully. The case does not directly tell us, but it is not hard to guess which parts of the vision achieved full implementation.

Is this a school district/community that is chronically resistant to change? The answer to this question would have to be no. We selected this district as a site for our Uses of Time study precisely because it has made a strong and sustained commitment to year-round schooling—an issue that has torn many communities apart. Forced into it by overcrowding, teachers, students, administrators, and parents came to like the year-round schedule and to believe in its contributions to strong student outcomes. This change was a huge structural reform dictated by circumstances that grew into a vision as constituencies evaluated its strengths and weaknesses. In this instance, the change *process* was consensual and the results endured.

PORTFOLIO PRISON—ESCAPE OR PAROLE

School Profile: Mayfair Middle School

Mayfair Middle School is a mathematics magnet school in a large southeastern city. The magnet program was created in the early 1980s as part of a systemwide desegregation plan. Located near the center of the city, Mayfair enrolls about 1,250 students in grades 6–8. A third of the students are minority, and just over half receive free or reduced-price lunches.

Under the original magnet school plan, Mayfair housed both the selective mathematics magnet program and a nonspecialized middle-school program serving students from its local neighborhood. Because few of the students who resided in the regular school attendance area qualified for the mathematics magnet program, the dual program strategy did not advance the district's desegregation goals. Recently, school policy has been changed to include all students who attend the school in the mathematics magnet program.

Mayfair's 75 teachers are organized into subject area departments and grade-level teams. Under the state assessment system, the eighth grade is an accountability grade, and there is considerable pressure on teachers in mathematics and English to ensure that their students do well. Eighth-grade mathematics teachers spent a lot of time mastering the new assessments. Early results from the assessments, particularly among students who had been classified as high achievers, were disappointing and resulted in frustration and concerns among the faculty. One issue that has surfaced is that eighth-grade teachers cannot bear the entire burden of the new accountability system. The mathematics content and instructional experiences that students have in sixth and seventh grades must also be aligned with the new assessments. An ongoing challenge facing the school is identification of resources (including time) and incentives to support and encourage all teachers to reform their classroom practices.

Case: Middle-School Mathematics Teacher

I am in the third year of my sentence in "portfolio prison." It has not been easy to accept my sentence of being an eighth-grade teacher in the state of Kentucky. The story of my incarceration begins in 1989. At that time, as a veteran teacher with 18 years of experience, I was confident that I had mastered the skills I needed to be successful in my classroom. Indeed, I was looking forward to relaxing and even allowed myself to begin thinking about retirement. Little did I know or even foresee the rude awakening that was about to jolt me out of my complacency and that would lead to my sentence.

In 1990, the Kentucky legislature enacted the Kentucky Educational Reform Act (KERA)—or "I don't care a . . ." as it is sometimes referred to by my colleagues in their moments of frustration. At the heart of this sweeping reform package is a new assessment system that includes state-mandated portfolio assessments in mathematics and writing. The accountability grades are 4, 8, and 12. (Recently, the state designated fifth grade as the accountability grade for the mathematics portfolios. The reason for this decision was to reduce the burden on fourth-grade teachers, who were originally required to conduct two sets of portfolio assessments.) Besides mandating the new assessments, the Kentucky Department of Education (KDE) announced that students' mathematics portfolios should meet the standards described in the *Curriculum and Evaluation Standards for School Mathematics*, published by the National Council of Teachers of Mathematics (NCTM) in 1989.

The publication of the NCTM standards alone provided a challenge and an opportunity. The challenge was to use the standards to guide my work in the classroom. This approach, in turn, created an opportunity to move away from what I was discovering had become a mundane curriculum and uninspiring teaching. For me, the challenge was to make the drastic change from a traditional lecture and textbook approach to one in which learning would revolve around the students' working independently and together. The mandated assessments added to the challenge, although I certainly did not always see them as affording any positive opportunities.

In August 1992, the usual nervousness that I feel at the beginning of a new school year surfaced right on schedule. Even though I truly love my profession, there are always conflicting emotions as the first day of school approaches. What kinds of students will I teach this year? Will I face my most "challenging darlings" in the last period of the day when my energy is gone and theirs is just beginning to surge? Will my most gifted students be open to exploring new ideas or will they stare at me as if to say "just the facts, ma'am?" What should I wear? How will I introduce myself? These are the normal first-day jitters. This time, there were other, more serious sources of anxiety—the mathematics portfolios and the pressure to deal with the NCTM standards. Of the two, the most pressing task was to implement the new portfolio assessments.

As the school year got under way, I had many questions about the new assessments: What is a math portfolio? Do they look like tests? Can I include dittos or word problems? Are they just files of student work? How will the portfolios fit with the rest of the curriculum? I did not have time to finish the textbook last year—when will there be time to do all of the new things? What can I discard from my regular curriculum? Can I use the activities in the NCTM standards for the portfolios? What about doing the portfolios as a project and getting them out of the way in a few months? Answers to these questions were hard to come by. Training and other support were limited. One of the few resources available to help get us started was a teacher's guide to creating portfolios distributed by the Kentucky Department of Education. This guide outlined only the barest essentials of the new assessments.

The school year passed in a blur. I went through the motions with my students, telling them often that the district had not really prepared the teachers to work with portfolios and that we would all have to do the best we could. As the year passed, I became more angry and resentful. How could the state and our own district leave us without any support? That the results of the portfolio assessments would be used to judge the schools and not the students only added to my anxiety. In my darkest moments it occurred to me that I could be fired just because my students did not do well on these new assessments, which no one I knew seemed to understand. Accustomed as I was to being successful in the classroom, I felt betrayed and abandoned. As the deadline for the completed portfolios approached, all of our work on the old curriculum came to a halt, and I spent most of the class time conferring with the students about their portfolios. The low point came on the day when the other teachers on my team joined most of the students on a field trip and I stayed behind at school to work with 12 students who had not completed their portfolios. Guilty! This was the beginning of my sentence in portfolio prison. In the months ahead, I felt as if I had to give up many things, including an enormous amount of time both in school and out of school, to work on the portfolios.

Later, in the spring of that first year, as I was scoring the first group of portfolios, I began to realize that my resentment of portfolios was influencing my students. In her introductory letter to a reviewer—a required component of the portfolios—one of my best students thanked me for concentrating on the textbook and not on the portfolios because "they were useless." Clearly my attitudes had rubbed off on my students and affected the quality of the work they were entering into the portfolios.

Near the end of the year, I began venting my frustrations to the principal. Most of my complaints were about the lack of training and follow-up support to help implement the new assessments. After one particularly loud outburst, the principal made several quick telephone calls. The result: I was named portfolio cluster leader for my school. My reward for complaining was more responsibility.

During the next year, I participated in a number of workshops to prepare me for my responsibilities as a cluster leader. These sessions helped explain what was to go into the portfolios (no dittos or worksheets) and how to use the rubrics to score the entries. They also introduced a number of sample activities. My immediate task was to communicate this information to my colleagues. As I discovered during the next several months, the combination of training my colleagues and experimenting in my own classroom helped me to become more comfortable with the portfolios. Gradually, these sessions with my colleagues evolved into a powerful tool for deepening our understanding of portfolios and the concepts embedded in the NCTM standards.

Three of us met every 2 or 3 weeks, as time permitted, to brainstorm ideas, plan activities, and assign ourselves specific development tasks. Finding the time was difficult, but the collaboration was critical. We developed strategies for managing the portfolios, became familiar with the scoring rubrics, and shared ideas about classroom activities. We tested new lessons and shared the results. Our experiments with new class projects led us to recognize the need to move away from the textbooks and to rely more on the new activities we were developing. This initiative involved more use of manipulatives, more reliance on cooperative learning tasks, and more use of students' out-of-school experiences as the content of mathematics lessons. For me, one of the most difficult lessons was to learn to worry less about correct and incorrect answers and to worry more about helping students learn to think and express themselves mathematically. Writing about mathematical solutions was a radical departure from how I was taught mathematics.

The second year ended on a positive note. After lengthy discussion and deliberation, the math teachers in my school awarded six portfolios a distinguished rating—the highest possible rating. We were exhausted but exhilarated. I would never have imagined that having a distinguished portfolio—not to mention six distinguished portfolios—would be such a momentous event. Our team was particularly gratified that one of these portfolios had been prepared by a student who had struggled all year. She had seemed unable to master traditional algebraic concepts, despite many hours of after-school tutoring sessions. She worked hard on her portfolio, choosing her entries carefully and writing articulately about her solutions and how she arrived at them. Two years of frustration, pain, and personal and professional anxiety began to fade as our team shared our student's disbelief and then excitement over her portfolio's distinguished rating.

The third year of my sentence is passing quickly. Portfolios have become almost a routine part of my curriculum, although I still spend a lot of time scoring the written pieces. The paperwork is endlessly time-consuming. There is still a struggle over what content to drop as I continue to add new components to the curriculum.

Has it been worth it? I am not sure. I have come to see portfolios as valuable tools in my classroom, although this view has come at a price. My school district and the state could have introduced the reforms more slowly and with much more support for those of us who would be held accountable once we implemented the reforms. The stress and frustration among teachers have been great. Each year, the eighth-grade teachers look around at their colleagues and wonder who the next one will be to request assignment to a different grade level or to a different subject area. I do not have a lot of hard data, but my clear impression is that many veteran teachers are requesting assignments away from the accountability grades and subjects.

Looking back, I am a survivor. My survival has been made easier by the opportunities to work with my colleagues. We were determined to master the new assessments. My sentence in portfolio prison continues, but parole appears to be a possibility.

Commentary: Curriculum Specialist

As a former eighth-grade teacher, I can identify with this teacher's frustrations and concerns. It is also clear to me, based on my more recent experience as a mathematics portfolio resource teacher for the same school district, that this teacher's experiences are typical of those of many teachers who are trying to implement these new assessments.

Overall, implementing KERA has had a positive impact on mathematics learning in many of Kentucky's schools. The schools have been forced to reexamine their mathematics curricula with an eye on content and instructional practices. As this teacher noted, time has been a critical issue in the reexamination. Teachers have had to learn that they can no longer begin the school year on page one of the textbook and continue working through the book until the year is over. They have also had to learn to abandon some standard practices, such as administering end-of-the-chapter tests. Instead, teachers are learning that the new assessments demand new instructional strategies and that the task of creating portfolios must begin early in the school year and continue throughout the year.

Teachers have also learned—often to their chagrin—that working with portfolios is very time-consuming. Ideally, teachers will review and critique students' work as it is completed. This process permits teachers to gain immediate feedback on their teaching. Using student work as a base, teachers can see where changes in what and how they teach can be made. In addition, as students revise their portfolio entries, they have more opportunities to learn.

Embedded in the new assessments is the very important issue of teacher accountability. Under KERA, schools receive rewards or sanctions based, in part, on student performance. Thus, the contents of student portfolios are seen as a direct reflection of classroom learning. Obviously, much of the quality of the portfolios is dependent on instruction and on teachers' mastery of content. In Kentucky, the standards for mathematics are based on the NCTM standards. Many teachers were unfamiliar with the standards; consequently, they faced the challenge of learning not only a new perspective on mathematics but also new ways of teaching mathematics. This was and continues to be a very difficult task for many teachers.

Commentary: Principal

"Portfolio Prison—Escape or Parole" is more than a description of an individual teacher's attempts to deal with change. It is a microcosm of the stages of any mandated reform in our schools and classrooms. Teachers often lack the training necessary to provide them with the information and skills to carry out the mandates. In my 23 years in education, I have seen many examples of reforms that get ahead of teacher preparation. In the case of KERA-mandated portfolio assessments, the Kentucky Department of Education (1992) guide was the "best" source for guidance for teachers, but its focus was outside of the classroom context. Generally, the lack of adequate resources to support teachers results in the confusion and resentment described by the case writer. At the same time, this is the point at which we can separate the professionals from those who use their problems and failures as reasons for giving up.

The second year of the case teacher's efforts to implement portfolios was marked by the resources that should have been available during the first year. As a cluster leader based at the school, the teacher became the school's resident expert. Her presence in this role was an important impetus to change. In effect, an external mandate became an internal task and there was sufficient expertise to carry it out. This teacher was able to spread her ownership of the task to other colleagues and to communicate her skills and knowledge to them. Through the collective activities, she was able to receive support and encouragement from her colleagues.

The third year finds portfolio assessments a well-integrated component of this teacher's classroom repertoire. Implementation has been a 3-year process, a fairly short period for such a fundamental change. The rapid pace can be attributed almost solely to the teacher's willingness to (1) participate in professional development activities, (2) recognize and acknowledge her responsibilities to carry out the mandate, and (3) collaborate with her colleagues. If she had failed to do any of these, implementation of the new assessments would be far from complete.

Commentary: State Education Department Official

This case describes the frustrations that arise when a teacher is thrust into a massive statewide reform initiative such as KERA. Teaching is a demanding profession, and KERA has upped the ante by asking even more of teachers and by holding them accountable for providing it. As this teacher reports, the first year of implementing the portfolios was a tough and uncertain time for many teachers at the accountability grades. Although Vermont's portfolio assessment system offered a number of important lessons, there were no roadmaps for anyone to follow.

The Kentucky mathematics portfolio system was developed by a statewide committee of leaders in mathematics education, many of whom had already been experimenting with portfolios. The committee intended that the new accountability system would fully embrace the spirit and goals of the NCTM standards. For teachers who were already attempting to teach to the NCTM standards, the portfolio system sanctioned their endeavors and allowed them to showcase their students' efforts and achievements. For other teachers, the KERA mandate forced rapid and, for these teachers, unanticipated changes.

From the outset, staff in the Kentucky Department of Education realized that the introduction and use of portfolio assessments in mathematics would be difficult. The portfolios represented not only a new way of thinking about assessment but also a new way of thinking about content as reflected in Kentucky's standard for proficiency in mathematics. From the beginning, we encouraged teachers to focus on the benefits of students' keeping portfolios, as reflections of students' achievements as learners. We tried to downplay the accountability issues.

Beginning in 1992, the KDE and its assessment contractor, Advanced Systems in Measurement and Evaluation (ASME), provided a variety of training and professional development opportunities to help teachers implement the new assessments. For example, in the spring of 1992, there was a statewide telecast that featured teachers and students who were using portfolios, along with commentary from Phil Daro of the New Standards Project. The video was rebroadcast the following fall, and schools were encouraged to use it as springboard for discussion. In addition, KDE and ASME organized and trained a state network of regional coordinators and cluster leaders who were to be responsible for training cluster teachers in using the new assessments. Along with the training, KDE and ASME produced both the *Mathematics Portfolio Teacher's Guide* (1992) and a second telecast. Finally, many districts augmented these activities with their own training sessions tailored to local needs.

One of the most important lessons that we learned is that teachers need a considerable amount of time to construct meaning for the portfolio process. For many, the time to commiserate with their colleagues was a turning point as a school faculty began to take ownership of the process. The sharing of management issues, lessons learned, and new instructional practices are all important by-products of this process. As this case suggests, one important and satisfying benefit of the hard work and time was an increase in the number of "distinguished" portfolios. Nevertheless, questions remain. Did the enormous investment of time result in large-scale changes in instruction and in increased achievement for all students? Is there more widespread analysis of student learning? Have the number of teachers who use portfolios in their classrooms and the number of students who are maintaining portfolios increased and spread outside of the accountability grades? In short, is the process shared by all so that the school has created a portfolio culture rather than a portfolio prison?

This case also suggests several important questions for KDE and district staff. Was the overall package of professional development and other support adequate? Were critical components of the support not available to this teacher? If they were not available, were the problems in access, information, or a lack of resources?

Analysis: Editor

The implications of a reform strategy that places extra burdens such as portfolio assessment only on teachers at certain grade levels are interesting. The writer of this case suggests that one result of the new policy is staffing shifts (one presumes statewide as well as in this teacher's district) into grade levels where there is less direct accountability for student outcomes. What patterns might emerge from this trend? Several possibilities come to mind:

- Portfolio grade levels may have younger, less experienced teachers as faculty with the most seniority defect to other grades.
- Portfolio grade levels may have the best teachers as faculty who are less committed to educational improvement and less willing to invest time to learn new strategies bail out.
- Portfolio grade levels might become the most collaborative because of the shared responsibility and challenge of the portfolio requirement.

Readers will no doubt think of other possible outcomes that might emerge.

The teacher in this case talks of the training that she received as portfolio cluster leader for her school (albeit a bit belatedly). Although she does not say so directly, we must presume that at least some of this professional development activity either involved time she would otherwise have spent in the classroom or required voluntary investment of after-school time—probably some of both. Release time during the school day generally costs the price of a substitute teacher, and funds for this purpose are usually limited. From a financial perspective (remembering that time is money), limiting the grades in which portfolios are required to four keeps down professional development costs. One wonders, however, whether teachers at other grade levels are being denied the opportunity to learn about an assessment tool that some argue is more effective for monitoring week-to-week student progress than it is for large-scale, statewide accountability systems.

Finally, this case is noteworthy for the stark contrast between a front-line teacher's perception of the adequacy of supports for reform and that of an individual at considerably more remove from the implementation process—in this instance an official of the state department of education. Understanding that KERA asks a lot of school staff, the state has conscientiously incorporated professional development and training into its educational reform plan. From the local implementation perspective, however, the support that the state has offered to ease the transition to portfolio assessment (which is only one of many KERA reform components) is minimal and hardly adequate to cover a teacher's question about "What do I do on Monday?"

FROM DEDICATION TO DESPAIR

School Profile: Cabot Middle School

A 5-year-old magnet school in a midwestern city, Cabot Middle School currently serves about 300 students in grades 5–8. So far, it has been able to accept all applicants. The student body is somewhat more nonminority and less poor than in the district overall. Nevertheless, it serves a healthy cross-section and tends to appeal particularly to students and families who are looking for a high degree of hands-on learning and more flexibility than traditional middle schools offer. The achievement of eighth-graders on stan-dardized tests is significantly higher than the national average.

Cabot offers a community-based, experiential educational program. It has a home base in a downtown building, but students and teachers often spend part of the school day at other community learning sites. A combina-tion of block scheduling and division of students and teachers into "houses" ensures that everyone rotates through the various learning sites, each of which is associated with a particular area of study, in the course of a school year.

Teachers work in two-teacher teams. The "houses" are mixed age and each student has an individualized instructional plan. Students have community-based mentors, peer tutors, and apprenticeship experiences.

Cabot had a rocky start and is still a work in progress. It went from being a plan on paper to full implementation with students in residence in a matter of weeks. Teachers spent the first 3 years literally developing cur-riculum a day before it was delivered. Cabot is also designed to be self-governing, meaning that a substantial amount of after-school time is devoted to meetings. Initially, teachers had few leadership or decision-making skills that allowed them to govern effectively and efficiently. As a result of all of these factors and others, teacher turnover was very high in the early years.

Teachers at Cabot also have less planning time than their peers at other district schools—a tradeoff for smaller classes. The school day for teachers and students is longer than at other schools by 30 minutes in order to "bank" time for 5 additional professional development days beyond the 5 that are in the union contract.

In addition to the case that follows, the first case in Chapter 3 was writ-ten by a teacher at Cabot.

Case: Middle-School Teacher

Shortly after graduating from college, I landed my first (and so far only) teaching position at a school that is truly on the cutting edge of innovation. Three and a half years later, I still believe in this school's unique philoso-phy, but I am seriously questioning whether I have the energy, stamina, and resiliency to continue to meet the demands this school places on teachers.

Our school, which is community-based, was the "brainchild" of mem-bers of the local business community. The mission statement says that the school's purpose is to "create an environment where the larger community collaborates to provide the expertise, resources, and community learning sites to help every child grow to his/her full potential." Its creators envisioned a school that depended on the community to provide the materials and resources necessary for children to learn. The school's philosophy embraces "hands-on," experiential education where students learn by venturing out in the community rather than by reading about an idea or a concept in a textbook. The community is the classroom. There is no reason to have textbooks or a library within the school when all resources are available in the community.

I wanted to be in a position where I could make a difference. This school would allow me to have a hand in constructing what I thought education should be for middle-school students. With only 225 students, nine full-time teachers, and approximately 15 support staff, there were opportunities to experience many things. When we began, there was no prototype or existing curriculum for our school. The teachers became creators and developers as well as deliverers of curriculum. We were also partakers in and of the learning experience and, with such a small staff, we played multiple roles. Here I was, so early in my career, having a real voice in the refinement and further development of this important institution.

How enticing a program like this was, especially to me as a first-year teacher. I was eager to work, but even more excited to be a part of this innovative, "latest" model of education. In the interview prior to being hired, the interviewing committee asked whether I understood that working in a school like this required a great deal of time and energy. I remember saying that not only did I understand but that I realized that extra time came with the job. After all, in college, we were told that it would be unreal to think that we would not take work home with us from time to time. I already knew that, in the field of teaching, I would work more than the 40 hours per week in my contract. So the idea of devoting extra time and energy did not alarm me.

From the outset, I epitomized the dedicated and committed teacher. I was the person who said during the assignment of tasks, "I'll do it." And the thing was, I really did want to do "it." I wanted to be a part of all the workings of the school. I thought that it was necessary to be involved so that I could understand the program thoroughly. The more I knew, the more I could help this school reach its vision of being community-based.

During my first year of teaching, I certainly taught, but I had many other responsibilities as well:

- Chairperson for staff development
- Contact for multicultural, gender-fair, disability-aware committee
- Liaison for an adolescent development program
- Contact person for the social studies team
- School contact for a state educational effectiveness program

- Building testing coordinator
- Supervisor for the production of the school yearbook
- Writer of graduation outcomes (our school was a district pilot site on outcomes)

All this committee work came on top of the usual responsibilities that all teachers have, along with some that are unique to our school: taking attendance, developing seating charts, putting up bulletin boards, ordering materials, honing classroom management skills, collaborating with my team member, creating and delivering curriculum, building relationships with students, evaluating assignments, and making community contacts.

As I look back on my requests for substitute teachers during my first year of teaching, I shudder. I was out of the classroom 21 days, none of which were for health reasons. My absences were attributable to meetings and workshops that I attended to glean information and knowledge to bring back to our program. "The more the better" was the philosophy. As a school, we tried everything and anything new. We exemplified experimentation and visionary thinking. We were "*the*" school of reform in the district, and our fame spread nationwide. Personally, I was showered with praise by my superiors and colleagues for my devotion and dedication.

Little by little, two things became clear to me. First, besides signing the usual union contract that protected me as a public employee, I had also tacitly agreed to an even bigger contract—the teacher dedication oath. This oath is unspoken, unwritten, and unsigned but morally binding. It reminds dedicated teachers that there is always more to do. It drives them to arrive early, leave late, and spend weekends "catching up" on work that was not completed during the week. Second, involvement in innovation can become a potent addiction. Once hooked, innovators find it almost impossible to give up or say no.

Because I am conscientious by nature, the oath of dedication and the endless innovative activity seemed reasonable at first. However, by the middle of my second year, I began to think that my "other" life was passing me by. I also believed that my primary role as an educator would be enhanced if I became more well-rounded. To accomplish this would mean less time working in and for school and more time experiencing other aspects of life. But I was faced with a hurdle: The teacher dedication oath gnawed at me. Would my conscience allow me to take a rest from my commitment to my job?

As time progressed, I actually became embittered. Why had there not been safety nets in place for me as a new teacher, to alert me to the warning signs of the innovation and dedication addictions? Teaching middle school is a hefty enough job. I know that new teachers are usually enthusiastic. Therefore, we are perceived as being capable of doing many, many things.

But there is a price to pay for being a new teacher who falls prey to the dedication and innovation syndromes so early on. There is the risk of burning out, potentially using up all of one's energy within the first year or two. By my third year of teaching, I was angry, exhausted, frustrated, and resentful. I knew that the quality of my work was mediocre because I was so tired. Could there not have been something in place to protect me from doing too much?

I know I could go elsewhere to teach. So why do I not leave? It is not that simple. I do not want to leave a program in which I have strong philosophical beliefs. My colleagues and I have built something together, and I feel a real sense of ownership and commitment. Also, some (myself included) might view leaving as "not cutting the mustard." But this type of program will continue to innovate and change, requiring resiliency and continued investments of time and energy on the part of teachers. Can I keep up my end of things? I do not know.

Commentary: District Administrator

I have worked in an urban school district for 27 years. I have been a classroom teacher in traditional and nontraditional environments. I have been a multicultural resource teacher. I have directed the public relations department for an alternative school program. I have written grants, developed curriculum, and created new assessment procedures. I have trained new and experienced teachers. I have supervised student teachers. Currently, I am responsible for the development of social studies standards for the district, including identification of a curriculum framework, recommendations for instructional strategies, and development of assessments that are aligned to the desired outcomes.

I provide this background for two reasons. In comparison with the teacher who wrote this case, I am a "veteran" teacher, with multiple experiences in the district. However, I am similar to the author in that time has been an important variable for all of the roles that I have played during my career. In different ways, to differing degrees, time has been an element to contend with and to learn to use to my advantage.

Everyone complains about time, not just teachers. Administrators demand more "quality time" and continuously look for creative ways to structure the day, week, semester, and year to buy them this time. Students say that too much time is spent at boring old school, but they also complain that there is not enough time to complete assignments, meet with their teachers, and participate in extracurricular activities.

I think that finding more time, even if this were economically feasible, is not the answer. Rather, we must learn to leverage the time that we do have. This, of course, is easier said than done. However, school reform efforts throughout the country do address the issue of time as they reorganize and reshape the institution of education. Examples of leveraging time include the following:

- Changing to a four-period day (secondary schools)
- Providing release time each week during which students work in the community and teachers have time to meet with peers
- Establishing collaborative teaching teams that may make more effective use of existing time
- Varying instructional strategies so that students feel that classroom time is productive and worthwhile
- Building in a reward system for staff members who work "above and beyond" the required school day
- Providing more autonomy for teachers because research shows that having control over one's work greatly reduces job burnout

These are not quick fixes. Schools are under increasing demands to do more with less. Students come to school with more social and economic needs than ever before. However, if we can learn to better use the time that we have, we may alleviate some of the genuine problems and concerns raised in this case.

Analysis: Editor

This case illustrates a potentially very serious problem in the educational reform context. We are heading straight for a time when significant numbers of veteran teachers will be retiring. Their positions will be taken by energetic and enthusiastic newcomers, like the author of this case. If, this time around, the momentum for educational change and improvement is sustained, these new teachers will be in danger of succumbing to the same kind of overcommitment that this teacher has experienced. Should the system be structured to protect novices from taking on too many extra-classroom responsibilities during their first years of teaching?

To answer this question, we must ask ourselves what we consider to be the primary responsibility of a teacher. Most of us would probably agree that it is to help students learn what they need to know and be able to do. Research has repeatedly demonstrated that perfecting classroom management and instructional organization is a pretty challenging task for the beginning teacher, who has probably had some student teaching experience and a few practicums but never full day-to-day responsibility for the learning and behavior of a group of children. How can you do this if you are running around to meetings instead of teaching or preparing to teach?

The policies and practices in other countries are instructive in this regard. For example, in Germany, prospective teachers student teach for 2 full years. In many German states, newly hired teachers (who are state civil servants) must spend a year or two as long-term substitute teachers who can be assigned to cover sustained teacher absences for reasons of illness, maternity leave, and so on. Through these policies, new German teachers gain 3 or 4 years of practical classroom experience before they are even eligible to be the teacher of record in a classroom.

In Japan, the initiation is different but still sends strong messages about the apprentice status of new teachers and their primary obligation to learn, above all, to teach well by the standards of the school, district, and nation. All novice teachers have one or more school-based mentors who take this responsibility very seriously. In addition, for the first year or two, new teachers are periodically released from their classrooms to attend district-sponsored seminars taught by experienced teachers. This support system is much appreciated by the novices, who express their reverence for experience and expertise in ways that would make us uncomfortable. Nevertheless, the contrast with our minimal attention to the nurturing of new teachers is striking.

We would argue that in the earliest years of teaching, veteran educators—both teachers and administrators—have an obligation to protect new teachers from themselves. When we look at the list of hats that this case writer wore during her first year of teaching, we are appalled. Even acknowledging that all staff must do many things because the school is small, new, and experimental, where is the logic in making a first-year teacher staff development chairperson or building testing coordinator? How can she know what needs to be developed? What the rules and procedures for standardized testing are? Without belittling her capabilities or squelching her enthusiasm, we think that someone should have been watching over her time and priorities.

CHAPTER 3

The Implementation Stage: Expanding and Testing New Ideas

The writers of the four cases in this chapter can all be described as teacher-leaders. In their respective educational reform contexts, they accepted the challenges of comprehensive school improvement plans and generously contributed their professional time to model innovative practices for their peers. After several years of heroic effort, each writer hit an implementation wall, in the sense that marathoners describe that moment in a race when they question their ability to continue the course. In one case—"Classroom Teaching and Professional Development: Must I Choose?," the writer takes us past her personal wall to a decision about the future. Would you have made the same choice? In the other cases, the writers' questions and frustrations are not entirely resolved. What would you do in these situations to maintain the momentum of school reform?

The writer of the first case in this chapter teaches in the same school as the writer of the last case in Chapter 2. Please refer to the School Profile for "From Dedication to Despair" as the context for "Teacher as Juggler." In addition, the commentary from a university faculty member that follows "Teacher as Juggler" may also be used as commentary for "From Dedication to Despair."

TEACHER-AS-JUGGLER

Case: Middle-School Teacher

Juggling. I threw the first yellow, balding tennis ball into the air from my right hand to my left, wondering what students would be thinking. I had not given them any directions other than: "Please be seated and ready to learn." The first ball I threw did not catch everyone's attention, but when I added a second ball, most everyone took notice as I began describing what they would be learning in class. The third ball I launched really caught their attention. Would I drop it? How long could I juggle the balls without making a mistake? Would I risk launching another ball?

Obviously, I use my juggling routine on the first day of class as a gim-
mick to hook my classes. I tell them that the three balls represent yourself,
others, and the world—what they will be learning about in social studies
that semester. But the juggling is more than that. It is a metaphor for my life
as a teacher, and as in juggling, timing is everything.

As a teacher, I juggle balls for a living—usually a lot more than three.
My school is an alternative, downtown middle school that prides itself on
being student-centered, experiential, community-based, project-oriented, and
highly computerized. We operate as a site-based management school. Our
curriculum is teacher-designed, teacher-written, and teacher-implemented—
no textbooks.

These are the basics of my instructional life: I teach three 12-week cycles
of social studies each year; the daily time blocks for my social studies classes
are 2.5 hours long. All classes are multigraded—that is, the students are a
mix of sixth-, seventh-, and eighth-graders. The curriculum is on a 3-year
cycle so that every student will have gone through each of the three social
studies courses by the time they graduate. In addition, I also teach other
courses for 2.5 hours per day for a total of 5 hours of direct student contact.

One ball that I juggle is a whole array of expectations, objectives, goals,
outcomes, standards, and skills that policymakers and the public have decided are the responsibilities of the schools—and, therefore, of the teachers. Educators—particularly at the middle-school level—are constantly mandated to add more courses (AIDS education, sex education, mediation,
recycling); subtractions are never mentioned. I can do anything, but I cannot do everything. There is not enough time.

Another ball that I juggle is constant curriculum development. That is
the nature of our school. My colleagues and I are always planning, creating,
writing, and piloting new curriculum. I have become a master at curriculum
evolution. I change assignments continually. Using my computer, I can change
a lesson, order copies made, and pass them out to students within minutes
when I sense it is necessary. Nevertheless, sometimes I think this incessant
curriculum innovation is a kind of insanity. It certainly takes time.

A third ball that I juggle is learning to teach in new ways. I admit that
I am not very adept with this ball. Mostly, I still stand in front of the class
and use basic classroom motivational techniques that I have picked up during the past 20 years of teaching. I know that I should be moving from a
teacher-centered, "I am the boss" kind of teaching style to a student-centered,
"how can I help you?" model. True, I do use the anticipatory set techniques
developed by Madeline Hunter, and I am alert to the many different kinds
of human intelligences identified by Howard Gardner, but no one has provided me with any research on how to meet the myriad and increasing teaching expectations within a normal day. I deliver a lesson, skill, or expectation and hope that students "catch" it. I worry about meeting the needs of

my students, who range from very needy learners to mature, independent thinkers who need greater challenges. Where can I find the time and expertise to deal with these issues?

Becoming a Better Juggler. Identifying and finding time within the contracted school day to talk, to plan, to create, to be a lifelong learner, and to teach gnaws at me constantly. It is not likely that things will change very much during my teaching career, so I guess I will have to learn to be a better juggler. There are things I can do, but others could help out too. Here are some ideas that I have thought about:

• My computer literacy skills have improved a lot since I began to teach at this innovative school, but they could get better. These skills make it possible for me to react more quickly in planning, creating, and delivering the teacher-developed curriculum that is a hallmark of our school.
• I should remember that I work in a relatively risk-free environment. It is okay to try and to make a mistake. Permission to make mistakes supports relationship-building by putting teachers and students on the same level as experimenters. I am experimenting and creating new curriculum as students experiment and try out their new-found knowledge and opinions about their world.
• I could advocate for a better way—a new teaching model. As a classroom teacher, I have too little flexible time for planning and delivering excellence to my students. A model like that of a college teacher, who has more flexible time and less direct time with students, would be one idea.
• I could get politically active. Until the public decides what they want from a school, we will have to continue to try to do everything. Boundaries must be set and the word *no* must enter the vocabulary of educators.

The teacher-as-juggler is not a new metaphor, nor is it foreign to other professions. However, within the present public school model, teachers seem to be increasingly unable to juggle the growing educational needs of students. Creating new models of innovative teaching will be difficult, but it is absolutely necessary if excellence is the goal and if our sanity is to be preserved.

Commentary: School District Administrator

It is rare, if not impossible, to find a teacher who does not feel greatly pressured by time. When schools struggle to do more with less, when demands for new curriculum ideas increase the already heavy teaching load, and when the needs of students demand more time from teachers, it is time that appears to be the villain. The writer of this case uses the metaphor of juggling to describe the constraints within which he works. Given the organization of the school district in which he works and where I am a district administrator, this is an apt metaphor. Our district has a mix of site-based and centralized decision-making structures that wear people down with too many meetings and a lack of clear decision-making focus. Furthermore, this teacher is constantly called on to toss one more ball in the air, without any staff development opportunities to improve his skills.

I suggest that although we may currently be using a juggling motif, our ultimate goal is a very different metaphor. As I envision balls being tossed into the air, I see them begin to blur, then become a seamless circle where one ball is indistinguishable from the other. Rather than individual balls circulating in the air, in constant danger of crashing down, I see a fluid lasso. The lasso is spinning quickly, but it is continuous and strong. This is my metaphor for a restructured school.

How can we move from the stress of juggling individual balls to my vision of a lasso? The answer seems relatively simple: The entire school day/year must be reorganized. Schools operate in a very old paradigm, combining the factory model with an agrarian calendar. In this day and age, this paradigm is simply dysfunctional. No other profession expects its employees to work steadily throughout the day without formal and informal time to meet with colleagues, solve problems, prepare for tasks, or mentor others.

But however simple the answer may seem, change involving the school day and year taps into deeply held assumptions and beliefs that make organizational change difficult. In our district, at least three barriers to changing educational time frames exist:

- *Money.* Taxpayers are not likely to increase taxes so that the school year could expand. The price tag is too high.
- *Teachers.* They are not happy with the system now, but they are not ready to give more time to a profession that is already burning them out. They would want assurance that change meant more for the better, not just more of the same thing.
- *Legitimacy of time.* There is an assumption that a teacher's "work" is teaching children. Time spent in staff development, teaming, or planning—that is, time when educators are not in contact with students—is suspect.

We may be juggling for a long time to come, but we need to at least begin to address the barriers, shift the paradigm, and get the balls spinning faster.

Commentary: University Faculty Member

I am writing this commentary from the perspective of a college professor who has had an enduring relationship with the school where the writer of this case, as well as the writer of "From Dedication to Despair," teaches. It is an urban middle school that was created as a collaborative effort between a large school district (40,000 students) and local corporate leaders. Initially, proposals were solicited from educators for a "state-of-the-art" urban middle school that used community resources to educate early adolescents. The proposal that was finally selected included such components as (1) multigrade groupings, (2) three community-based sites (an arts site, a science site, and a social studies/government site), (3) a trimester school year, (4) extensive use of community mentors, and (5) a "student-centered" curriculum with individualized learning goals.

This new school became operational very rapidly, opening with six teachers and a principal. These original six teachers were literally creating curriculum and school structure on a day-to-day basis. And they were working without a scheduled preparation period—a choice the staff made in order to maintain a low student/teacher ratio in their classes. By the third year of operation—the year in which the two teachers who prepared these cases arrived—none of the original teachers remained. They had created many exciting learning experiences for students, but the stress of constant curriculum development was simply too much. Ironically, the educational ideas that the school was attempting to implement have attracted national attention; as a result there has been a steady stream of visitors and observers—an additional source of stress.

Besides its uniqueness as a community-based school, this school sought to integrate elements of the middle-school model recommended by the National Middle Schools Association. These elements include a curriculum that is interdisciplinary and is constructed around the interests and concerns of early adolescents; "skills" instruction integrated into all classes; a variety of "options" and "electives" courses; and an "advisory" component for social/academic advising and "adolescent skills" instruction. Thus, besides curriculum planning and implementation, this philosophy asks teachers to give a great deal of time and attention to the emotional needs and social interactions of early adolescents struggling to form an adult self-identity.

Innovative middle schools such as this one attract some of the most creative, dedicated, and talented teachers in the profession. As this case writer points out, such teachers can teach anything, but they cannot teach everything. Furthermore, such teachers can teach anything by any method, but it takes time and practice to do it well. However, the majority of teachers presently implementing the middle-school concept were themselves schooled in traditional junior high schools and trained at the university level to teach their content area specialty. They have to learn how to do things differently. The success of a curriculum or instructional approach is greatly influenced by the degree to which the teachers have achieved mastery over the theory and process. Curriculum ideas must be understood so completely that they can be expressed simply and concretely to students. Instructional processes must become automatic and natural. This kind of mastery for teachers is developed over time, through practice, through sharing with other teachers, through a process of personalization.

Time is what teachers need, but time is precisely what we do not give them.

Analysis: Editor

There is a weariness to the tone of this case that is dispiriting. Here is a very experienced teacher who chose to help develop a potentially exciting experimental program, but the bloom is obviously off the rose. While he describes the many balls that he juggles, I suspect that the heaviest ball to bear is the curriculum development one. When a program design calls for nearly total abandonment of off-the-shelf curriculum materials, teachers are faced with a lot of work. Further, in its earliest days, this program took an existential leap from a design prepared by one group to full implementation by another. The implementers had no time for their own planning or to practice what they would be preaching—and no curriculum. That set of circumstances represents a teaching marathon. Anyone would be exhausted.

The case writer's idea about a teaching model with more inherent flexibility is an interesting one. We have recently been studying the culture of a small group of elementary schools where teachers have considerably more daily and weekly planning time than is the norm. While this study is not yet complete, we think that we are seeing relationships between control of time, fluidity of time, and the level of stress and harassment that characterizes a school's ethos. There is never enough time, but when time is fixed and chunked by external forces, it becomes the enemy. When it can be constantly molded and adapted to fit individual and group needs, it becomes an available resource.

RECLAIMING REFORM

School Profile: Tobias Middle School

In the mid-1980s, Tobias Middle School was considered one of the worst at its level in a large eastern city. Today, it is one of the best—a citywide magnet with a sizable waiting list.

Tobias serves 550 students in grades 6–8. Its student population is ethnically diverse. About 75% of the students qualify for free or reduced-price lunch, and 23% have special needs. The school has a staff of 65. Teaching faculty are supported by a number of unusual, specialized nonteaching positions such as cluster leaders, an evaluation team leader, a director of operations, a student support services coordinator, and an administrative support specialist (community liaison). The specialist roles, which are filled by certified teachers, are designed to free classroom teachers to focus on curriculum, instruction, and student achievement.

The focus at Tobias throughout the restructuring process has been on improved student achievement. On 4 days of the week, students attend school 1.5 hours longer than other middle-school students in the district (which accumulates to 36 additional school days per year). The extra time is devoted to supplementary periods in reading and math. Writing is taught in every subject area, and a study-skills program reinforces academic work. Faculty are also working on development of an interdisciplinary curriculum.

Teachers and students at Tobias are organized in grade-level clusters. Teachers have unusually large amounts of common planning time, including 2.25 hours every Friday afternoon when students are not present.

The extra student contact time associated with Tobias's program requires extra resources—approximately $9,000 per year per teacher. In the current climate of fiscal restraint in education, the program's future is not assured.

Case: Middle-School Teacher

Genuine reform requires that educators lay intellectual claim to a new paradigm and reconstruct their previous patterns of action to realize it. Habit and vested interest in familiar behavior patterns seduce our allegiance to new paradigms and erode our will to implement them. Hence, claiming and realizing reform is only the first step. Educators must persistently reclaim their vision for a new educational paradigm and reevaluate the degree to which their daily activities embody it, if reform is to remain vital over time.

It was the dog days of August. My wife and I, both teachers, savored the remaining days of summer vacation while counting down to the first day of school. Returning east from visiting family, after having finished dinner in Chicago, I called our answering machine. The first message was the voice of the eighth-grade cluster coordinator at my middle school. He conveyed the surprising and welcome news that I would be an English teacher in his cluster the coming year.

As the train sped eastward, I lay awake in my berth that night remembering my excitement 3 years earlier when I was hired by the school-based management committee of my school, the flagship middle school of our school district. Project Promise, our school's innovative reform program, has received the National Excellence in Education and the A+ For "Breaking the Mold" awards from the U.S. Department of Education. The school is an intersection of numerous collaborations among local private sector, nonprofit, and educational institutions.

Our school day is extended by two periods to double the math and reading periods Monday through Thursday. Reading, writing, and math are taught across the curriculum. Teachers, organized in grade-level clusters, have two common planning periods a day (three, if a 50-minute block of time after student dismissal is counted) to create and monitor the teaching of interdisciplinary, thematic curricula. Clusters are coordinated by teachers released from classroom responsibilities who facilitate planning, maintain contact with families, provide discipline support, and expedite communication between teachers and administrators.

Project Promise reforms in organization, teacher time, and curriculum, together with associated payoffs in student achievement, made my move to the school a quantum career leap. The school's program, values, and mission were perfectly matched with my own commitment to "grass-roots" curriculum development, cooperative learning, and team teaching.

Also in August, 3 years earlier, the school principal had asked whether I would develop a critical-thinking curriculum and teach it as a creative writing program using computers. Because my own undergraduate and graduate education was in philosophy, I leapt at the chance. I was pleased to be able to translate some of the best current educational theory into practice.

Three years later, my critical-thinking curriculum was in place, and I had survived the transfer from a Wang system to a state-of-the-art Macintosh lab. However, as the critical-thinking teacher, I had been a member of the specialist teacher cluster that met only two periods a week; the special classes we taught provided the time for the three academic clusters of teachers, on separate schedules, to meet and plan curriculum together. Although we specialists synchronized some of our curricular efforts, we envied the common planning time that academic cluster teachers had each day to create thematic, interdisciplinary curricula tailored to the needs of their students. Thus, I welcomed the opportunity to join an academic cluster at the beginning of my fourth year.

The eighth-grade cluster was reinventing itself as I entered it. Scheduling for a large class required administrators to divide the eighth grade in two, a larger and a smaller cluster, each on a different schedule. Other teachers besides myself, some of whom were new to the school, were added to these clusters. We added a second cluster leader, and I became the English teacher in the smaller cluster. The different schedules of the larger and smaller clusters allowed us to meet together as one eighth-grade cluster only twice a week for 50 minutes. Given this schedule, interdisciplinary curriculum planning had to be done separately by the two eighth-grade clusters. Standardizing curriculum content and synchronizing instruction could be done during our limited common meetings. However, clusterwide curriculum planning did not occur in the common meetings of the two clusters nor in those of my smaller cluster.

Academic cluster meetings in the original Project Promise reform were never intended to be devoted solely to curriculum planning. They were also meant to provide opportunities for teachers to assess the academic and behavioral progress of students and to brainstorm and share strategies that would enable students to excel. Conferences between parents or guardians, teachers, and students could also be scheduled at these times.

These uses of meeting time are important and necessary. However, as the first marking term wore on, I grew increasingly eager to begin the process of creating curriculum, the task that I had read about so enthusiastically 3 years earlier in preparation for my job interview. When I finally asked whether we were going to do this during common planning periods, the response from coordinators and colleagues was sympathetic but noncommittal. The reason curriculum planning had not begun, they said, was that meeting time was short and there were many other things to do. There was simply too little time, they thought, to jointly plan curriculum.

On Fridays, students are dismissed early, and the three hours remaining for teachers are devoted to professional development. If scheduled planning time was insufficient, I suggested, why could not our cluster coordinators help arrange, in consultation with administration, to allocate two Friday afternoons a month for curriculum planning. The coordinators replied that two common planning periods a day were already scheduled, to say nothing of the 50-minute block after student dismissal; the administrators said that if teachers were unable to accomplish Project Promise goals by meeting once a day, they then should avail themselves of the other scheduled time, which was not being used for curriculum planning.

My cluster did not discuss the issue further at the meetings, and business resumed as usual. Conversations with members of the two eighth-grade clusters convinced me that other colleagues shared my concerns. However, these teachers observed that our existing meeting time had to be better organized before we could talk about curriculum planning. If meetings were run more efficiently, they said, colleagues would be more receptive to resurrecting common planning time and, perhaps, to expanding it.

At my cluster's next meeting, I suggested that we formulate long- and short-term goals, determine the necessary steps to reach them, and create a time line. A cluster leader suggested that the three other weekly meeting times each be used for a specific purpose: one for curriculum planning, one for discussion of student discipline, and one for discussion of students' academic progress. This was a start. Maybe one period a week spent planning together would inspire us to spend more. However, when the meeting designated for planning rolled around, "business as usual" prevailed.

When I observed, a short time later, that we still were not doing common curriculum planning, the response from cluster leaders and almost all colleagues was again sympathetic. Some still observed a need for more planning time in the schedule. They maintained that there was not enough time for common planning, even though scheduled time was not used for this purpose.

At this point I stepped back to reflect on why common curriculum planning was not happening. The reorganization of the eighth-grade cluster placed teachers new to the school and teachers new to each other as cluster colleagues together for the first time. Did we need to do more to create what military theorists call "small-unit cohesion" before curricula could be produced? On the other hand, would not collaborative curriculum planning engender cohesion? Commitment to planning interdisciplinary, thematic curricula seemed stronger for some than for others. What could we do to enhance understanding of and commitment to this mode of instruction? Did the absence of a production schedule account for our slowness in getting on with actual planning?

Organization theorists make much of the difference between the formal ways in which an organization is supposed to operate and the many informal ways in which it actually does operate. Progress in reclaiming reform in schools does not always occur in the manner or within the time frame we expect, even if it is consistent with our intentions. This point was driven home to me over the next couple of weeks in several ways.

As I speculated on why some teachers believed that time for common curriculum planning was insufficient, the science teacher in my cluster pursued a comment I had made in our cluster meeting. I had observed that the annual science fair projects provide a natural opportunity for common planning; they are tangible intersections of the major subject areas for which science teachers too often bear almost sole responsibility. He and I agreed to meet and plan collaborative student projects. As we talked, the comment of a younger and wiser member of the cluster came to me: "Just begin doing the new thing with another person; don't wait for others to buy into the idea!"

The wisdom of this remark was further revealed to me when three bilingual teachers in my cluster described how they were conducting alternative assessments for their students. They had met intensively, including two or three weekends, to hammer out the logistics and materials for this radical shift in their own and in their students' way of doing school. Here was collaboration, common planning, and innovation right under my nose! These teachers had made common planning time out of their own time because of their commitment to improving their methods for evaluating students. How could their willingness to collaborate, plan, implement, and monitor be spread so that time already made for common planning could be so used?

About this time, we began as a school to implement a district mandate to teach interdisciplinary curricula. As a curriculum on hunger was being refined and taught, I heard more teachers extolling the virtues of interdisciplinary curriculum planning. Awareness was growing among us that, rather than just adapting a prefabricated curriculum, we could create and tailor curricula to the interests and needs of our students.

I revived my earlier nomination of science fair projects as natural and convenient opportunities for interdisciplinary cooperation, and I proposed that we in the smaller cluster devote a week to these projects. Usual classes could be suspended and students divided into groups based on their progress on their projects to date. Our ultimate goals were for individual projects to show improvement, for students to gain deeper understanding of science as an intersection of all subject areas, for teachers to collaborate, and, equally important, for students to see teachers doing so. My proposal was unanimously accepted.

This is how things stand now. Some Project Promise ground—in common curriculum planning—has been reclaimed. And it is clear that reform and innovation in our school (and probably in others) must be reclaimed year-to-year and sometimes month-to-month. Slippage into old and familiar patterns of behavior—say, individual instead of cooperative curriculum planning—is as possible as genuine progress.

Clear also is that it is naive to assume that simply reiterating the reform paradigm will effect intellectual assent and behavioral compliance. It is more realistic to expect that once the reform has gained a concrete foothold here and there, others will try it because it looks good. It is at this point that a clear presentation of the virtues of the reform—for example, of teacher-created, thematic, interdisciplinary curricula—may encourage the skeptics to embrace it.

The most innovative and empowering changes do not have lives of their own; these changes must be reappropriated each year by teachers and administrators. The hard question is "How?"

Commentary: Principal

Reading this case caused me, the principal of the school discussed, to feel a mix of emotions. First, I felt despair in response to the case writer's feelings of frustration. I was profoundly disappointed to realize how this teacher's enthusiasm for reform had been dimmed by the tenacity of business as usual. Second, I felt guilt for not having mandated that faculty give top priority to curriculum planning during their cluster's common planning time. As the school's principal, I could have easily delivered such a mandate.

Ultimately, I realized that one important aspect of school reform is teacher empowerment. At our school, it is—and I believe it should be—teachers who decide how to use their planning time and what their planning priorities will be, based on the needs of the students they serve. Engaging in the education reform process causes teachers to experience both anxiety and growth. Organizing and managing the school so that teachers help guide and engage in the reform process also cause me to experience both anxiety and growth. But I have the expectation and the confidence that teachers, as professional educators, can and will make the necessary adjustments to better serve our students. Moreover, making hard choices about just how to do that will allow teachers at our school to develop to their full potential as educators.

The question that looms and lingers in my mind about this case is: What are the priorities of the teachers and clusters in our school, and how are those priorities determined?

Commentary: Assistant Principal

As an administrator in the school described in this case, I have observed that what drives cluster teachers to devote planning time to curriculum design is the interest of an individual or small group of teachers in teaching a special thematic unit or in accomplishing a specific instructional task. Although such interest is an excellent catalyst for compelling the teachers in a particular cluster to focus on the development of new and innovative curriculum, it is not an effective way to drive schoolwide reform. Curriculum development is far too vital to take a "back seat" to pressing daily issues; it should not be on hold until someone comes up with an idea for a thematic unit.

In most successful, progressive ventures, it seems, an individual or a few individuals take the lead, working diligently to build and sustain momentum. This, I think, may always be necessary if we are to sustain the practice of continuous curriculum planning at our school. For as the case writer observes, teachers may slip into old and familiar patterns of behavior, especially veteran teachers who have achieved a fair degree of success with tried-and-true instructional methods. Strong, intentional efforts to improve the status quo will probably always be needed.

Consequently, I think it is incumbent on school administrators to take a stronger lead in ensuring that curriculum planning becomes and remains a top priority. First, we in administration should make faculty assignments so that each cluster has some teachers who will ensure that cluster time is used effectively and that it has a deliberate focus on curriculum planning. Second, we should mandate that each cluster devote a specified amount of time to curriculum planning each week.

Revising, enhancing, and creating new curriculum and instructional strategies must be a priority if we expect to adequately prepare students to meet the challenges of the 21st century. Therefore, it is imperative that administrators make curriculum planning a top priority for teachers and that we create and protect time for curriculum planning within the school day.

Commentary: Teacher

As I sit at the hair salon Saturday afternoon, locked under the hair dryer for a solid undisturbed hour, I am determined to read and respond to the case so patiently awaiting my review. The cover letter establishes that I am already 2 weeks overdue in submitting my comments. As I read further into the case and establish that the focus is on teacher time as it relates to interdisciplinary curriculum planning, I have to chuckle. I gaze at the bag of journals across the room, eager for their turn under the dryer with me. I envision another bag in my entranceway at home that contains neatly labeled folders of the past week's work, equally desirous of my attention and comments. I recall the half-completed batch of standardized test materials being compiled for my reading classes; because I have one week until that activity takes place, it did not make the list of work to be toted home this weekend. When, indeed, do we plan and implement interdisciplinary curricula?

The school discussed in this case has made the commitment to establish and protect time to scale the mountain of interdisciplinary curriculum planning. What a wonderful place to work. How nice it must be to have time to perfect thematic units that connect all subject areas. Before I can fax my resumé, however, I realize that I am already employed by this school, and that my esteemed colleague—the case writer—has captured the essence of our interdisciplinary curriculum planning dilemma quite precisely.

Like us, teachers in many schools, I suspect, often find themselves too busy bailing out the water to plug the leak in the boat. We must make choices. My classroom instruction time—which I prefer to use to engage students in probative, analytic discussion—is not used for "busywork," the traditional means at a teacher's disposal for obtaining time to review and assess student work. I must find other time for responding to the written work my students produce. Telephone calls to parents and correspondence with community members also take a cut from the school day. Students' individual problems, concerns, and questions require immediate answers when they arise; they do not wait for a regularly scheduled time. When teachers cluster, these issues plus those regarding alternative means for dealing with certain students' difficult behaviors take precedence. This is the "business as usual" that the case writer correctly observes has priority over common curriculum planning.

The evidence of recent research strongly suggests that interdisciplinary, thematic units do much to facilitate the learning process for students. Once introduced to a topic, students can share their knowledge in other classes and apply it in different ways. They gain confidence from using and extending their developing frameworks for knowing. These benefits are reason enough to reclaim the Project Promise reforms. The pressing question is when.

School and district administrators can be helpful in addressing the question of time. Even though the case author and countless other teachers (including myself) do huddle together with one or two other teachers periodically to formulate interdisciplinary units, common planning time as a recipe for curriculum reform must be a much larger undertaking. Recently, our district administration mandated that each cluster conduct a 2-week interdisciplinary unit on world hunger. We may do it whenever and however we choose, but each cluster must submit weekly instructional plans that reveal the content of each subject area within the interdisciplinary unit. This mandate is a directive from above requiring us to plug the leak in the boat amidst the bailing of water. I do not suggest that administrators should always mandate the topic of thematic units, but periodically assigning a week or two to thematic, interdisciplinary instruction is helpful. It actually supports us in work we know to be important, but that is difficult to accomplish amidst the crush of daily life in schools.

Analysis: Editor

This case is of particular interest on two counts. First, it represents a rare group of public schools where the quantity of time in school has actually been increased for both teachers and students, with concomitant increases in teacher compensation. Second, it is both old and new enough as an innovative school to be grappling with the nitty-gritty dilemmas of the concept of continuous progress. There is plenty of evidence in the case that this school has been restructured: grade-level clusters with common planning periods, cluster coordinators released from teaching duties, an extended school day. There is also evidence that the original vision has not been entirely realized, particularly the parts related to curriculum.

In the early 1990s, two big ideas about curriculum made their way into many, many educational improvement plans across the nation. One idea was curricula organized around themes. The second idea suggested that, in the absence of published thematic, interdisciplinary curricula, teachers should become curriculum developers themselves. The appeal of interdisciplinarity is undeniable. As adults, we all know that the problems and issues of daily living and working rarely sort themselves into neat bins where we can discretely apply what we learned in English, biology, or American history to reach a solution. As real-world problem solvers, we sort through the array of knowledge and skills that we have acquired over a lifetime of learning to find an appropriate solution set for a particular situation. Why not directly teach students to approach issues in this way from the outset?

The question of whether teachers can or should be curriculum developers—especially developers of interdisciplinary curricula for which there are few high-quality models to serve as referents—seems to be problematic. Even in a school like this one where extra time and creative scheduling produce relatively extensive common planning periods for grade-level teams, teachers shy away from the curriculum development task incorporated into their school improvement plan. We suspect that they do not feel up to the task, and probably rightly so. It is one thing to pull together materials from a variety of professionally developed curriculum sources into an instructional unit; teachers routinely do this. It is quite another to outline scope and sequence and write the material yourself. That is a full-time job that cannot be adequately done in 40-minute segments.

This school successfully implemented many aspects of its original reform plan and has improved student outcomes to show for it. At this point, it would probably be wise for administrators and faculty to revisit that plan to update and clarify what remains to be done. This would provide an opportunity to discuss what "teacher-developed, thematic, interdisciplinary curriculum" means to individual faculty members and to reach some consensus on continuing commitment to this goal and the investment of time that teachers are willing to make in achieving it.

DUAL-LANGUAGE DILEMMA

School Profile: Habanero Elementary School

Habanero Elementary School is located in a predominantly Hispanic, working-class neighborhood of a large southwestern city. The school has an enrollment of about 800 students, of whom 88% are Hispanic and 92% receive free or reduced-price lunch.

Several years ago, this school became part of the Accelerated Schools Program developed at Stanford University and began a restructuring process designed to address four critical problems identified by the principal: (1) low motivation in both teachers and students, (2) low expectations for students, (3) low student achievement, and (4) low parent involvement.

The restructuring plan focused on introducing more challenging curriculum and varied approaches to instruction; in-school and after-school enrichment activities for students; school-level decision making by faculty and administrators, including hiring authority; and strategies to increase parent involvement. Specific features of the restructuring included some mixed-age classrooms, portfolio assessment, a greater emphasis on use of technology, an in-school enrichment program on Friday afternoons, a low-cost after-school program staffed primarily by teachers 3 days a week, and a parent center staffed by two social workers. In addition, the school committed itself to honoring diversity and promoting bilingualism among all students.

Teachers at Habanaro have wholeheartedly embraced the school improvement efforts. Most have volunteered a great deal of personal time to supervise the after-school program, develop enrichment classes, and participate in the many meetings associated with a self-governance model. They have been gratified by some positive results, such as a reduced student mobility rate, fewer discipline issues, and greater student self-confidence. In addition, there is some evidence that test scores have improved significantly for dominant-English students. Evidence is more limited with regard to outcomes for limited-English-proficient students, who are generally not required to take state and local accountability tests. However, several years into the restructuring process, signs of burnout were beginning to appear.

Case: Bilingual Teaching Team

Our school is a pre-K through fifth-grade elementary school. During the past 10 years, the neighborhood around our school has changed considerably. Most of the white, middle-class residents have left, and they have been replaced by a rapidly increasing population of blue-collar workers and laborers who are predominantly Hispanic. The student population at our school reflects this change: approximately 90% are Hispanic.

Our decision to develop a two-way bilingual education program for our second-graders grew out of our desire to more effectively meet the academic needs of our growing monolingual, Spanish-speaking student population, and at the same time to help our English-speaking students acquire a second language—a necessity for the 21st century. Our school's traditional bilingual education program, which ends in the fourth grade because there are too few bilingual educators available for the intermediate grades, had been only partially successful. Many of our students were leaving our school at the end of fifth grade with limited English skills, despite the efforts of our bilingual teachers to turn monolingual Spanish-speaking students into speakers of fluent English. Our goals were to honor the two languages and to increase verbal communication by team teaching—one of us in English and the other in Spanish—and by increasing the opportunities for interaction among English-speaking and Spanish-speaking students in the classroom.

We believed that this approach would help both groups of students to learn a second language more quickly than they would in a traditional classroom.

Our classroom was designed to accommodate 40 students—20 monolingual Spanish speakers and 20 monolingual English speakers and limited-English speakers. We created an environment that was conducive to flexible grouping and team teaching—small tables, rocking chairs, rugs, and books in both languages were everywhere in the room. We developed the dual-language program entirely on our own time. We worked primarily after school and on weekends, and we implemented different components of the program as we went along. We researched the topic extensively, and we also learned a great deal about organizing and implementing the program from one of our fellow teachers who had grown up in Central America and who had been educated in a two-way bilingual program throughout her entire elementary and secondary school career.

Developing and implementing the program was a challenging experience. For example, one feature of our program requires students to read the same stories in both languages. Often our English-language materials had to be translated into Spanish—a burdensome task that we reserved for weekends—because it was difficult to find a sufficient number of high-quality Spanish-language books and other resources. In addition, at the beginning of the school year we spent a great deal of time meeting with the parents of our English-speaking students, many of whom did not understand why their children should spend class time learning Spanish, "the language of the poor." We had to work hard to convince some of them of the importance of knowing a second language.

Our two-way bilingual program is now in its fourth year. Our bookshelves are filled with Spanish and English books, and our walls are decorated with posters in both languages and pictures that reflect both cultures. However, we still struggle to find time to do all that is required: meet with parents to allay their fears and explain the goals of the program, translate materials into Spanish, and develop lesson plans that allow students to develop competence in their primary and secondary languages while learning mathematical concepts, science, and social studies.

Despite these difficulties, the program has been a success. Because we have created a warm environment in which there are many opportunities to learn in both languages—and avoided instruction that emphasizes drill and repetition—students have become less inhibited about communicating in their second language. The results have been particularly impressive among our Spanish-speaking students. We have found that they are generally more motivated to learn English than are their English-speaking peers to learn Spanish. In our view, this difference in motivation is quite understandable.

Not only are monolingual Spanish-speaking students constantly exposed to English-language television, newspapers, and other forms of American culture, but their parents often encourage them to develop English-language skills so that they can help the family carry out daily routines, such as shopping, banking, and taking public transportation, and live a better life in their new country. Among the monolingual English-speaking students and their families, learning Spanish is still considered an enrichment activity; for the Spanish-speaking students and their families, learning English is viewed as a necessity for surviving in the United States.

Although all students appear to have benefitted from such activities as reading and listening to stories in both languages and from working in small groups with classmates who speak both languages, we have found that our Spanish-speaking students are more inclined to take the risk of writing in their second language. During writing workshop, most Spanish-speaking students prefer to write their stories in English, even though they have the option to write in Spanish. On the other hand, the English-speaking students typically do not elect to write their stories in Spanish; they are more disposed to practicing their Spanish-language skills in conversations with their peers during the many small-group activities that are planned.

Unfortunately, our students' continued progress and success have been limited by the fact that the dual-language program does not extend beyond the end of the second grade. There are two main reasons why teachers in the upper elementary grades are reluctant to form pairs in order to create dual-language teaching teams. One is a lack of understanding of how the program works in practice and a lack of opportunity and time to learn about the development and implementation process. (Not everyone is willing or able to sacrifice their personal time—as we did—to this endeavor.) Second, there is the fear that, under an arrangement in which teaching occurs in both Spanish and English, teachers will not have enough time to develop students' English-language skills and adequately prepare them for the state and national tests they must take in the upper grades. This is a particularly strong concern because our teachers feel some pressure to meet the unrealistic goal of having all of our students fluent in English by the time they enter middle school.

Some teachers argue that it is easier to implement a dual-language program in the primary grades because there are few time pressures on teachers to prepare students to take standardized tests. In addition, they maintain that, because there is less content to cover in classes, such as social studies and science in the early grades, it is much easier to integrate the various subjects and teach both languages at this level. New teachers in particular often feel that they need to prove themselves by having their classes perform well. They are concerned that teaching the same material in both Spanish and English takes too long and makes it that much more difficult to cover all the required class material.

Teachers in the upper grades fail to realize, however, that, despite some of the new demands placed on our time (translating materials, doing joint planning), our team teaching allows us to teach more efficiently and effectively. For example, in a regular bilingual education classroom, the teacher must remember to speak in both Spanish and English. Invariably, one of the two languages is used more than the other. Because we team teach in Spanish and English, we know that each language is getting equal time and that our students are getting maximum exposure to both. Team teaching also increases our opportunity to work with small groups or with individual students who need additional assistance. For example, while one of us is teaching a lesson to the whole class, the other is free to assist those who need extra attention.

Perhaps the most important reason to offer a dual-language bilingual program, however, is the fact that by the 21st century all children will find it necessary to speak more than one language. Our dual-language program is only a small step in promoting the schools of the future. Our vision is to see all children study two languages throughout their entire school career. However, we suspect that teachers at our elementary school are not unique in their reluctance to implement a program like this in their classrooms. In fact, for the reasons stated above, resistance is likely to be even greater among middle-school and high school teachers.

Many students in other countries receive such an education with no apparent ill effects—our colleague being one. This approach to education can work, and work well. Unfortunately, like other attempts at reforming our education system, we have run into the barrier of time. Our fellow teachers recognize the importance and effectiveness of what we have accomplished in the lower grades and have been very supportive of our efforts. However, they are unwilling, or perhaps unable, to make the necessary changes themselves.

Commentary: Principal

The challenges described in this case serve to highlight three additional issues that I will discuss briefly.

First, although this case describes a "dual language dilemma," it also describes the "duel" between and among languages that tends to occur most often in Florida, Texas, Arizona, and California—states with large numbers of non-English-speaking students. We must learn to reexamine seemingly discrete and independent subjects, tasks, and activities, and begin to build and nurture relationships among "shareholders"—all who care about teaching and learning. Schools are complex, yet they consist of interdependent parts. There are time requirements and time limitations; constantly changing structures, roles, and responsibilities; and a host of activities that occur simultaneously. It is therefore imperative for us to learn how to simplify tasks and foster relationships. Success in any one area cannot be achieved independently of the entire community of learners.

Second, the case writers imply that there is a need for teachers to think about the entire education system. Their awareness of the need for students to be able to speak more than one language in the 21st century and their understanding of the value of creating curricular and other linkages between and among elementary, middle, and high schools as a means of promoting and enhancing student achievement indicate that they are systemic thinkers. It is imperative that systemic *barreras* (barriers) to student achievement be identified and removed, and systemic thinkers within our schools can help to make this happen.

Though less obvious, this case also draws attention to the issue of equity. Local, state, and national government agencies will often target resources—funding, time, and talent—to help new suburban communities become established by developing needed infrastructure and providing essential services. Unfortunately, this outpouring of resources by government agencies does not happen in many other communities that have experienced a different kind of population shift: an increase in the number of poor and limited-English-proficient residents. In many of these communities, resources such as funds, time, and talent are not redistributed to the schools that students from these families attend. This difference in resource distribution helps to ensure that students living in poor, resource-starved areas will never achieve on a level comparable to that of their peers in more resource-rich areas. Is America not interested in the "redistribution" of academic achievement among students in different communities, just as it is not interested in the redistribution of wealth?

Commentary: Teacher

As a teacher of third- and fourth-grade students at this elementary school, I applaud the dual-language approach as a model for preparing our students to function successfully in the academic world and in the larger society. More than two-thirds of my third-grade class this year came to me from this program. Rarely have I received students as literate and intellectually enthusiastic as these children, and, as a result, I have no reservations about the quality of the language instruction in the primary grades. My perspective on the reluctance of teachers in the upper grades to implement a dual-language program is, however, somewhat different from that of the case authors.

There is a limited number of qualified bilingual teachers throughout our state and within our school. As a result, our school provides bilingual teachers to our K–4 classes only. Unfortunately, bilingual teachers who are assigned to the upper grades are often reassigned to the primary grades when our school experiences an increase in student enrollment. This reassignment occurs because bilingual instruction is viewed as a higher priority for students in the lower grades. Even if enough bilingual teachers were available, however, the philosophical orientation of many of these teachers would make the implementation of a dual-language program nearly impossible. Traditionally, students who receive bilingual instruction are taught in their first language for most of the day, with only about 45 minutes reserved for instruction in English. Many bilingual teachers, who are convinced of the value of this method, are resistant to any changes. In other words, it does not matter how open I am to attempting a dual-language approach in my classroom; I have no Spanish-speaking counterpart willing to complete such a team.

Resistance to dual-language instruction among intermediate-level teachers is not the result of pressures related to standardized tests per se. Rather, the teachers' resistance is rooted in their knowledge of the reality that faces students who are classified as limited-English-proficient when they enter middle school. These students have very poor prospects. First, they are not allowed to choose electives—English as a Second Language is their only "choice." Thus, they are excluded from the music, fine arts, and technological courses that are available to their peers. Furthermore, they are routinely placed in less academically challenging courses. The negative effect that such placements can have on students' future achievement prompts teachers in the upper grades of our school to push for "English at all costs."

We can hope that, as our middle schools pursue current restructuring efforts and as additional research on second-language acquisition becomes available, it will become easier for teachers in the upper elementary grades to introduce a dual-language program. The benefits of this approach are obvious to those of us who have observed the program. Now we need the resources to implement this effective approach and the confidence to believe that such an undertaking will do no harm to our children.

Analysis: Editor

The writers of this case contributed a good deal of their professional time to develop and pilot a creative and apparently successful approach to bilingual education. Their curriculum and instructional strategies clearly demonstrated to students, parents, and colleagues that facility in more than one language is valued and valuable. However, the fact that other teachers in the school have not rushed to replicate their achievement is not unexpected, for reasons that they cite and other reasons as well.

American ambivalence about the value of fluency in a second language is well known. Politically, we are still debating policies to entrench English-first or English-only rules that deny the importance and validity of other languages. If anything, our xenophobic tendencies are more prominent than ever in the mid-1990s, as both federal and state governments rush to enact legislation barring even legal immigrants from the rights and services conferred on citizens. This is not a ripe time for tolerance of diversity.

If some educators in this district are committed to the value of second-language learning for all, perhaps they should pursue a political and public relations approach that emphasizes (1) the positive outcomes of two-way bilingual education for students who speak English as their first language and (2) the broadening of career opportunities for individuals who speak multiple languages. Given the current scarcity of teachers who are fluent in two or more languages, a short-term strategy might be to collect several of those who are bilingual into one or more magnet schools or programs in the district where the strengths of the dual-language approach could be pilot-tested as students move up through the grades. The general trend toward waivers of policy, including state testing programs, for experimental and charter schools might give a pilot such as this a "hold harmless" period of time to get started.

On the other hand, state and local policies often deliberately exempt or exclude special populations such as non-native English speakers from testing programs for various reasons, including an assumption that the language barrier will result in low individual scores, which in turn will lower classroom and school averages. If the two-way bilingual instructional approach is as promising as it appears, its proponents might strengthen their case for universal bilingualism by seeking a waiver specifying that all students enrolled in classrooms or a magnet school using the strategy must take state and local tests required of monolingual English-speaking students. Average or better test scores under these conditions would be a powerful argument for second-language learning.

In terms of teachers' professional time, any effort to expand the dual-language appoach—whether in this school or in a magnet—should give serious attention to finding the time and money to support the identification or development of appropriate curriculum materials in both languages. It is unrealistic and inefficient to expect that all teachers can successfully develop a program and deliver it to students at the same time, as the case writers have.

CLASSROOM TEACHING AND PROFESSIONAL DEVELOPMENT: MUST I CHOOSE?

School Profile: Palmetto Elementary School

Palmetto Elementary School is located in a suburban area of a large city in a western state. It is a K–5 school, serving over 800 students, approximately half of whom are from minority backgrounds, primarily Hispanic. The faculty includes 26 regular classroom teachers and 2 special education teachers. The official district student-teacher ratio for the elementary school level is 31:1. Enrollment at this school is growing, and several classes are housed in portables and trailers on the campus. There is a bilingual class at each grade level.

Palmetto has a continuous-improvement plan that is reviewed and updated regularly by a school site council composed of the principal, teachers, and parent representatives. Teachers also collaborate through grade-level teams. The district has a new language arts core curriculum. Therefore, the most recent improvement focus has been on literacy, particularly in the early grades. Among other things, considerable effort has been devoted to involving parents in the literacy development of their children. Other recent professional development emphases include performance assessment (including portfolios), hands-on science, and a self-study of the history–social science curriculum.

Case: Classroom Teacher/Mentor Teacher

When I became a fourth-grade teacher 11 years ago, my expectations were high. I wanted to be the best teacher I could be and I wanted to make a big difference in the lives of the children I taught. In my classes, learning would be fun as my students learned about the world around them and did not just memorize facts. One of the first things that I learned was that my own education, particularly my professional training, had not equipped me with the skills I needed to reach my goals. I was surprised—often overwhelmed—by the diversity of the students in my classroom. Some had trouble reading even the simplest passages; others were beginning to give up on learning and school altogether. What I needed was a curriculum and some instructional strategies that would help me meet their diverse needs and get them hooked on learning.

Fortunately, help was not far away. In 1984, my first year of teaching, I attended my first Activities for Integrating Math and Science (AIMS) workshop. The purpose of this two-day workshop was to help teachers explore and understand the possibilities for integrating mathematics and science. By giving us the opportunity to experience the mathematics and science activities just the way our students would, and by modeling a variety of hands-on teaching and learning activities, the training encouraged us to depend less on textbooks and traditional instruction. Here, I thought, was at least the beginning of a strategy for meeting my students' diverse learning needs and interests. We heard reports that other teachers were trying these new ideas and getting great results. There was much to learn and much to try. I returned to my class once again determined to make a difference.

Back in my classroom, I quickly discovered that what had seemed pretty clear in the training was, in fact, very complicated. Moreover, there was a risk. The textbook was safe and secure. Developing my own curriculum and materials was not. I plunged ahead by adding math games to our classroom activities. I reasoned that if my students were having fun, they would be more likely to learn the concepts and facts I had built into the games. Later, we began exploring the world of our school and our neighborhood through simple observations and experiments. The students were becoming scientists. Gradually, I began to see changes in my students. They were learning more, and they seemed more sophisticated in their understanding. Most important, they enjoyed learning.

During this period my own joy in learning about teaching increased. As I grew more confident in this process, I started to work with another teacher, and we began to share our ideas with our colleagues. Some of them resisted, but many joined us in our discoveries and experiments. The two of us were able to continue the process by attending more workshops and institutes. At the end of our third year of teaching, we decided to take an even bigger step by applying for a joint mentor teaching position in our state's Mentor Teacher Program. Following our successful application, we spent a considerable amount of time working with other teachers in our district to introduce them to AIMS activities and cooperative learning in math and science. Because the district had only six elementary schools, we were able to provide training and other kinds of help to all of the teachers in the district. We also learned even more about the benefits of teachers' being able to work together for their own professional development.

After my fifth year of teaching, I moved with my family and found a job in a much larger district. The principal urged me, before leaving my old school at the end of the year, to get "involved" quickly in my new school and district if I wanted to work for change. I volunteered for committees and worked hard to learn about the district and its approaches to education. After 3 years, I once again applied for a mentor teaching position in my school. To my great surprise, I was hired as a district mentor and charged with the responsibility of providing professional development and writing new curricula in math and science. The district had, in effect, hired me as a classroom-based teacher trainer.

Preparation for my new responsibilities included many workshops in math education, particularly on the emerging state mathematics framework. Moreover, there were trainer-of-trainer activities and an array of institutes in all areas of the curriculum and on student assessment. Although the training prepared me to be a trainer, it also led me to try many new things in my classroom.

Looking back, I see that this was a very productive and rewarding time. It was also a very busy time. Two other teachers and I worked on new curricula for the district, and we prepared other teachers to use it in their classrooms. In addition, we worked on new performance-based assessments and helped our colleagues introduce them in their classrooms. I had three roles: learner, teacher, and teacher trainer. All of them were exciting, challenging, and rewarding. Each of them took an enormous amount of time. I realize now that I was making, and continue to make, very difficult choices.

The main drawback to my professional development activities with my colleagues was that I was spending 20 to 30 days a year away from my own students. At first, it was only a day here or a day there, but gradually the amount of time increased. My own training took up some of the time, which in turn helped me improve my own instruction. The rest of my time was spent with other teachers or working on curricula. Gradually, as my time away from class increased, I began to feel guilty. Was this fair to my students? What had happened to my earlier professional goals of being the best teacher I could be and meeting the needs of my students? I wondered if I could be as effective a teacher if I were not challenging myself to be a learner. I did not want my enthusiasm to die or my teaching to become routine. And I continued to worry about what my students were missing.

The parents of students in my class were also concerned about the amount of time I was spending away from my classroom. They complained to the principal, saying that my first priority should be my students. My principal backed me and my work. She reminded the parents that I was a better teacher because I was learning about teaching and spending my time implementing new programs. Despite her support, I had my doubts. Perhaps I was stretching myself in too many directions.

What was I willing to give up? I could give up the classroom and devote my time to professional development activities and curriculum development, or I could give up my role as a mentor and spend all of my time in the classroom. I wondered if I could be effective as a teacher trainer if I were not trying things in my own classroom. I also wondered if my excitement about trying new things in the classroom was influenced by the training that I was getting and by the opportunity to share the experiments with my colleagues. These were difficult questions for me, and, in the end, I could not make a choice. Instead, I looked for some middle ground.

I realized that I needed to do a better job of helping parents to understand the need for ongoing learning opportunities for teachers. It is important for them to understand the changes that are going on in their children's classrooms and to know that teachers who are prepared to work with these changes are going to provide better education for their children. A second possibility would be to use my classroom as a demonstration site for other teachers in the district and perhaps even for observation by student teachers. This arrangement would allow me to remain active with my colleagues without as much time away from my students. A third possibility would be to redefine my job so that I teach part time and work as a teacher trainer part time, splitting the school year into two parts with one devoted to the classroom and the other to teacher training. It would also involve splitting the week into several parts.

In the end, I returned to my original goal of being the best teacher that I could be. My experience told me that working with colleagues and developing new curricula and assessments improve my teaching and help me have an impact on education outside of my classroom. There must be a way to balance the daily demands of the classroom with the needs for collaboration and professional growth of teachers.

Commentary: Parent

Turning your child over to the care and responsibility of the person who is to be the teacher for 5 hours a day, 5 days a week, is not always an easy thing to do. As a parent, you want to feel comfortable and secure in the knowledge that this person will do the very best for your child.

My child was a student in this teacher's classroom. Throughout the year I took comfort in the fact that here was a teacher who was willing to take personal risks—in terms of exploring new ideas—to develop herself and to expand her range of skills for the benefit of my child and the other children in her class. I was also glad to see that the school and the school district were willing to support these efforts. My own memories as a student include being in classrooms where teachers never varied in what they taught or how they taught it. We were bored, and we could see that the teachers were bored, too. Looking back, I realize my time in school was not very inspiring. School should be challenging, and it should be fun for everyone.

Teacher absence for a few days out of the school year is no reason for parents to feel that their children are being cheated, particularly when the absence is for special development and training. In this case, most parents' concerns were eased by keeping us apprised of what was going on and why. More important, any parent who has had the opportunity to visit or, better still, assist in a classroom quickly recognizes that it takes much more than teachers' regular attendance, a textbook, and a few ditto sheets to hold students' interest and attention. Teachers should be encouraged to seek out fresh new ideas for their classrooms so that they can be confident and enthusiastic about what they teach and how they teach it.

Commentary: Principal

This teacher faces a difficult dilemma as she tries to resolve several critical issues. She describes herself as a teacher, a learner, and a teacher trainer. She cherishes each of these roles and recognizes their value for her continued growth and development. At the same time, fulfilling these roles takes her out of the classroom for 20 to 30 days a year—as much as one-sixth of the time available for instruction in our annual school calendar.

It is difficult for any teacher to be out of the classroom for long periods of time, and this teacher has been absent a lot. The immediate solution to the problem was for the teacher to look carefully for a skilled substitute and then to work with the substitute to ensure that she was adequately prepared for her classroom responsibilities. As it turns out, the preparation has been quite effective, and there appears to be little or no disruption of classroom instruction. I would also note that preparing the substitute was both an extension of the teacher's professional development activities and one more demand on her already full schedule.

Because of these efforts there have, in fact, been few parent complaints about the teacher's absence. Indeed, most parents respect this teacher and want their children assigned to her class; there have been no requests to have students transferred out of her classroom. Nevertheless, that teachers' time is pressured by competing demands for these various activities remains a source of concern.

Our district recognizes the importance of linking staff development and school improvement efforts. These links are critical to making schools better. We have also learned that many of our better teachers are effective trainers and coaches for their colleagues. We have come to realize that our teachers benefit from professional development activities that combine centralized—at the district level—training with on-site activities that include workshops and more direct over-the-shoulder help in their classrooms. We continue to experiment with different strategies for scheduling these activities. Thus, as in most districts, there are sessions after school, on weekends, and during the summer. In addition, we often make use of shortened school days for various kinds of training. We have not found a single best formula, but we have learned an important lesson about time and schedules: Professional development is most effective when it fits into teachers' personal schedules rather than the other way around. This approach means that professional development that is available when teachers have questions or are busy with development tasks and that addresses these questions and tasks will have a greater impact on teachers than professional development that reflects external decisions about both content and schedule.

Commentary: District Administrator

Concerns regarding use of time are particularly intense for teachers like this, on the edge of the transitional front, attempting to juggle doing the new and improved with the old and expected. Unfortunately, they find that doing everything that they want to do is not possible.

In education, more has historically been equated with better. Education promotes students' gaining more knowledge, covering more curriculum, preparing to achieve more or higher degrees. Measures of assessment have typically been indexes of quantity such as number correct or completed within time limits. This notion of quantity as an index of success misdirects teachers in their quest for improving their instructional strategies. In responding to and preparing our students for a technological society, I suggest that measures of quality, not quantity, may best define success.

Our state frameworks and other related documents challenge educators to prepare students for a future in which information is managed electronically, factory workers are in limited demand, and multiple careers are the anticipated norm. These frameworks call for classrooms with a thinking, meaning-centered curriculum, where students become cooperative workers, problem solvers, self-starters, and information managers. Current learning research reveals that a constructivist education yields significant advantages in developing depth of understanding and the ability to apply learning to future problem-solving and learning situations.

When teachers modify educational opportunities to meet these challenges and to incorporate these new understandings, they meet confusion and resistance from many of the groups to whom they are responsible: parents, administrators, and other community members. This teacher's parent education efforts seem an excellent solution to this problem. It appears she has resolved that what she needs is time better spent—not simply more time. She chooses to spend precious time educating her colleagues and her students' parents about the goals of their children's educational experience. This alignment of understanding reduces the pull from competing interests and allows her to focus and better use her limited instructional time.

Similarly, her professional development and role as a teacher educator cannot be generalized in a "more is better" fashion. This time problem cannot be solved by simply reproducing this teacher's experience for many or all teachers to provide a larger pool of mentors who share responsibilities and thereby reduce the strain on her time. This particular teacher was chosen by the district not only because of her professional expertise, but also for her exceptional dedication to her profession and her extraordinary interpersonal skills. It is the combination of these characteristics that makes her an exceptional staff developer and justifies significant district support. These traits also motivate her to ensure that the distractions and time demands of her role as staff developer have a minimal impact on her students.

Analysis: Editor

This case very clearly illustrates the tensions set up when teachers pit their own need to continue learning and growing against their primary responsibility for facilitating growth and learning in children and youth. As Hargreaves (1991) has observed, the result is guilt and a need for teachers to rationalize time spent learning to be a better teacher. To her credit, this teacher seems to have worked her way through the personal feelings of guilt to a balanced middle ground. She is fortunate to have plenty of support for the multiple roles that she chooses to play in her school and district. That is not always the case.

All the evidence presented in this case and in the commentaries that accompany it indicates that this teacher works in a very enlightened environment when it comes to educational change strategies. The state has provided a comprehensive framework for reform, grounded in research and current thinking about the work-force skills needed for the 21st century. Realizing that the new curriculum frameworks asked teachers to introduce more rigorous content and new instructional strategies, the state also created a mentor teacher program so that the most self-directed, intellectually curious, and confident teachers could help their colleagues respond to the new mandates. Obviously, the state also had a realistic time frame in mind for full implementation of its reform plan, since this teacher's participation in implementation activities has been ongoing for over a decade.

But even given a sound state policy structure for change, attitudes at the district and school levels have the most direct impact on an individual teacher's experience of the change process. Again, this teacher has been fortunate. The districts she has taught in have supported her desire to be both an excellent classroom teacher and a teacher-leader. Further, as the commentary from her current principal attests, the district's approach to professional development offers a nice combination of episodic events and sustained, school-based follow-up that has at least a fighting chance of drawing all teachers into the reform orbit.

Finally, we get a sense from this case that the multiple hats the author wears all fit very comfortably. I suspect that she is very good in all her roles—

a caring, competent teacher of young children; an attentive, open-minded learner; and an empathetic, dynamic teacher trainer. There is an interesting contrast between the equilibrium she has achieved in her very hectic professional life and the experiences of the equally busy but less satisfied teacher who prepared the case entitled "From Dedication to Despair." What circumstances might account for the differences in these two situations?

CHAPTER 4

The Continuous Improvement Stage: Keeping the Vision Dynamic

The final two cases in this book are about alternative schools that have been notable success stories for many years. The perspectives offered by the case writers are those of founding fathers who helped to craft the original vision of their institutions and have critically observed the impacts of shifting educational policy contexts over a long period of time. Both are unhappy with what the passage of time has done to their dream teaching situations. At this writing, both have left their teaching positions—one opting for retirement, the other for a leave of absence to try college teaching. These cases raise important issues about time, personal change, and institutional change. Does time inevitably dilute core reform principles? Can good ideas become too rigid?

QUALITY TIME IN AN ALTERNATIVE SCHOOL

School Profile: Allen Alternative Middle School

Allen Alternative Middle School is located in a large eastern seaboard city. Established more than 20 years ago, it serves just over 300 students in grades 6–8. Because the students are selected by lottery, Allen is more racially diverse than most schools in a city where housing patterns tend to segregate school enrollments. All of the school's students receive free or reduced-price lunch. Average daily attendance is 94%, far above the city average. About 90% of graduates go on to magnet high schools, many of them selective.

Allen's defining programmatic characteristic is mixed-age and mixed-ability classes. The school operates on a trimester system. Three times per year, students select their courses from a catalogue, much as college students do. Most classes are open to all students, regardless of age or grade. Exceptions are math classes such as algebra. Teachers develop and offer courses such as Great Debates, Music Is Communication, and Other People, Other Languages. Instructional strategies are varied and include cooperative learning groups, peer tutoring, and frequent forays into the community.

Another key characteristic of the school is site-based decision making, a privilege that it has enjoyed since its inception as a state-designated experimental school. By faculty agreement, teachers at Allen have always had fewer preparation periods and taught more classes per week than other middle-school teachers in the district, in exchange for smaller class size. Originally, students went home at 2:00 P.M. each day, allowing teachers an hour of common planning time per day; this luxury is no longer available.

Currently, the school has a special, experimental contract with the local teachers' union, allowing them to maintain their preference for fewer preparation periods in exchange for smaller classes. The union is leery of this arrangement, however. In addition, the district has mandated site-based decision making for all schools but has instituted a bureaucratic process for reviewing and approving school-based management plans. Despite more than 20 years of experience in this area, Allen faculty's first plan was rejected. Although it now has an approved plan, its requests for waivers (e.g., allowing students to be dismissed an hour early on one day per week) have been rejected.

Case: Former Middle-School Teacher

The Dream. For 20 years, I taught in a teacher's dream-come-true of a public middle school—a school built from scratch, where teachers, parents, and students formed a learning community. Teachers were given much freedom in selecting curriculum and in structuring their own and students' time. Designed in 1974 as an alternative setting for a maximum of 250 students who would attend by choice, our dream school offered these features:

• The school was located in the downtown area of a large city, with easy access to museums and other cultural institutions. It emphasized individualized/personalized learning and small classes.

• The learning community chose to have a trimester school year, with built-in time between trimesters for student and program evaluation, registering students for the next term, reorganization of newly formed classes, and teacher preparation of classrooms for new subject matter.

• Understanding the value of planning together, teachers chose to have common preparation periods at the end of the day. Parents agreed to have their children dismissed 45 minutes early each day so that teachers would have important planning time to evaluate programs and make ongoing adjustments.

• Teachers were given ample time to prepare thoughtful, comprehensive, essay-type evaluations for each child.

• Once a week, the school dismissed children at noon so that teachers could meet to discuss individual students and to share their classroom experiences of dealing with children who had learning problems, whether behavioral or academic. These shared experiences produced understandings that resulted in improved teacher/pupil relationships, which affected learning for the better.

• Students had a voice and many opportunities to practice making mature choices. Their voices were heard especially in monthly town meetings where they could speak openly about their concerns and make suggestions.

• Parents were encouraged to participate in making important organizational decisions.

So many of these uniquely local reform measures were possible because our school was designated "experimental." This status allowed us freedom from state, district, and teacher union regulations. Experimental status allowed waivers on all but the most basic academic requirements. The school functioned with truly site-based management long before this concept became a popular or mandated reform.

Change was a fact of everyday life in this evolving alternative program, and our professional time was under no less pressure than it would have been in a traditional school. Yet teachers found that when control of time was in their own hands, and when staff and students were able to make so many of their own choices—both curricular and organizational—there was much less resistance to change. The realization "if it doesn't work, we can change it" made all the difference. Had the changes been mandated from without, no doubt they would have been met with much more opposition. Staff drew energy because they knew that they had this wonderful, on-site freedom to make sensible changes within the unique community of students, teachers, and parents.

Trying to Keep the Dream Alive. Over a 20-year period, I have witnessed the gradual loss of a number of features of this great experiment. After a few years, a new school district administration failed to renew the school's experimental status, and the school had to conform to many of the traditional district and state requirements. Given a new school location and an additional 100 or more students, teachers had to cope with larger classes and found it more difficult to give individualized instruction.

Next, breaks between trimesters were eliminated. The staff held on to the concept of individual appointments for registration, but they had to conduct registration while the entire student body remained in school. Only half the teachers could be on hand in the registration room; the others had to be with the children in classrooms.

Eventually, the time that had been allowed for writing extensive student evaluations was reduced to the barest minimum, making it necessary for teachers to force-fit this critical activity into prep periods, lunch time, and—mostly—after-school hours. Despite losing the time they needed to best perform these activities, teachers again made the necessary accommodations in order to hold on to the dream.

Lost forever, I fear, is the unique feature that gave teachers a common preparation period at day's end, without the presence of children. This is generally looked on as "wasted" time in today's educational climate.

The weekly teacher meetings for the important and revealing discussions of individual children were also lost for many years. Just recently, however, this time has been restored, but only if teachers submit a plan that would make up for the displaced instructional time. To meet this requirement, we submitted a plan that involves special book report projects that students complete at home. (Teachers, of course, must monitor students' attention to the projects.)

Teachers at this school continue to innovate, but today they are more likely to do so because they have to rather than because they decided to. As I write these words in the school library, there is a faculty discussion going on about the use of portfolios in the evaluation of student performance. The state's outcome-based education plan calls for all schools to use this device. I heard several teachers at the meeting make excellent presentations of how they are trying to incorporate this fine learning tool into their classrooms. One teacher remarked that although she felt confident in the completeness and worthiness of her students' portfolios, she had no idea where she was going to find the 15 minutes needed to analyze the contents of each of 130 portfolios and then to blend this analysis with other evaluative criteria to create a comprehensive evaluation of the student. Others seemed overwhelmed at the thought of just maintaining the folders while attempting to keep up with all the other aspects of classroom life.

There is a sense that we do not control our time or our program as we used to. The pressure mounts on us to do great things without the time to do them well. But although the faculty continues to hold on to the dream of providing extraordinary, personal, individual attention to each child, there are signs of stress. Two teachers retired early; two younger ones have indicated plans to retire even earlier; and there is talk of early burnout among others.

What Lies Ahead? I am one of the teachers who retired early, but I have not really left. Instead, my solution to the frustrations of trying to provide personalized instruction was to act as a volunteer tutor in this school where

I taught for so long. The freedom to set my own agenda has made it possible for me to work with students on a one-to-one basis; I fit into classrooms where I feel I can function best and generally make myself available to individual students who seek help. There is time to get to know each student as a whole person with interests, hopes, unrecognized talents, and a unique personality. So much of knowledge and deeper understanding tends to flow naturally in such informal, one-on-one meetings. A class size of one is the ultimate in individualized education.

Obviously, this solution is not open to everyone. It made sense for me because I had done my "time." But what about the young husband-and-wife team who are contributing so much, yet plan to move on to other pursuits? When questioned about their reasons for leaving, they agonizingly replied, "Not enough time—to prepare for classes, to give attention to student papers, to communicate with other teachers, to share information with parents, to devote to our own children. Time is moving too fast!"

Because a new principal has brought fresh ideas and obtained much in the way of updating the program with high-tech equipment, this school has improved over the past several years in many ways. The school has reapplied for renewal of the experimental status that had given it so much flexibility in the past. Yet the question remains: How can such a program continue to give quality time to each student within the time constraints and reform mandates placed on teachers from within and without? Different people offer different options:

• Politicians and the public seem to think that adding more time to the school day and year would result in more learning. When one considers a "normal" school day's workload for both staff and students, fatigue and frustration would seem to make this solution questionable at best.

• Another option is to apply to become a charter school, under the new federal policy of allowing local school districts to grant schools the kind of autonomy our school has traditionally valued.

• One possibility is to give students more responsibility on portfolios by allowing them to analyze and report on their own progress.

• Perhaps, if they could find the time and resources, the faculty could meet to creatively explore solutions to the time problems. Maybe they could agree to drop some activities in favor of others, such as teachers' planning time. More planning time for teachers usually means more quality time for students.

In raising these issues, I hope that teachers in other places will join the discussion and submit their own ideas. If enough of us speak up, maybe the system can change.

Commentary: Teacher

In this tale, note the ticking of the clock. That is what it is all about—that devil time. I admit that I am half of that couple mentioned in this case who are seriously thinking of an early (mid-forties) retirement. Why? We enjoy the students and staff. We like the challenges and small successes of every teaching day. We just do not have time to breathe, to be with our own children, to smell the flowers in our nonexistent garden, or to do the kind of volunteer work in the community that the author now does by serving as a tutor at our school.

As a teacher, I get half an hour not to eat lunch and 45 minutes to "prepare." Those times are filled with making telephone calls, writing interim and final evaluation narratives, arranging trips, and filling out forms. I coach a chess team and, very occasionally, say "hi" to my colleagues. I must be prepared before I arrive because a prep period is never spent prepping. Once, I got to see the teachers' lounge! What are the effects of this rush? Imperfect worksheets, little time for individuals (students or colleagues), planning in isolation, and only pretending to give my attention to some things.

But the gigantic problem of time pressures is bigger than the school system. Western culture is obsessed with time. Our bias rewards those who view time as important. Only those who are out of the mainstream, like the elderly and the homeless, have time on their hands. Yet, we have generations—sorely needing a chance to communicate with and care for each other—who are kept apart by our various social systems, including the schools.

I am glad that the author of this case, an ex-teacher, gives of himself to show that he cares about the students. The time that he spends offering encouragement to students and engaging in conversation with them certainly does a world of good.

It is worth noting that there are many people like him who could also serve children with proper encouragement from schools, from children, and from our government. Maybe requiring hours of parent participation in the school (like the co-op school I used to know) is an answer. If it takes a whole village to raise a child, why are we locking the doors and keeping too many people out of their children's education?

Teachers and administrators need to demystify education and to welcome the community into our buildings. They can help us, they can help students, and they can teach us something about the community as well. Although community involvement in our school cannot ease all the pressures that I feel, I should not have to retire to find the time to get to know my community.

Commentary: Teacher

This case raises an important point about the perceptions and attitudes of American society toward the purpose of schools. It seems to me that the majority of our society sees school as a holding place for children, not as a place that embraces society's children with nurturing love, discipline, and knowledge. The idea that teachers could use time without students to do more for students is one that is difficult for some administrators, parents, and other members of society to accept. Instead, time spent on activities like writing extensive evaluations of students, common preparation time, and early dismissals to allow whole school professional development is generally perceived as "wasted" time for students.

I am a teacher myself, and in my opinion, changing people's ideas about what teachers do and when they do it will be difficult to accomplish. Teacher time is usually perceived as what can be done during the relatively short school day. But a good teacher who is doing a good job cannot shut down when the 3 o'clock bell rings. The public needs to know that the job of teaching children exceeds the day defined in the teacher contract. A good teacher calls parents, plans lessons, plans trips, researches materials, duplicates materials, changes classroom displays, writes recommendations, writes midterm reports, grades papers, writes report cards, among many other things. It is not possible to fit all of these tasks into a 6-hour time period and to interact with 120 children a day (as we do at our middle school). And, should a school want to continue to make changes to improve education, that requires even more time for planning and implementation.

To be truthful, many teachers should rethink the time commitments in their jobs. Teachers should view themselves as professionals, such as doctors and lawyers. Teaching is too important to be left to anybody but the best and the brightest. Teachers should go into the profession knowing that their day will definitely extend beyond 3 o'clock. But they should also be compensated like other professionals who put in long hours. Teacher salaries should be high enough so that they do not regard what happens after 3 o'clock as unpaid work. In other words, the perception of the legitimate teacher day needs to be extended. It is only then that I think the problem of teacher time will be solved.

Commentary: Principal

The situation that this case documents suggests to me that educators should be looking beyond their own realm for new professional models. Standard practices from other fields should be reviewed for their potential applicability to the teaching profession. Doctors consult outside office hours. Lawyers research cases in preparation for pending litigation. It does not, then, seem unrealistic for us to consider that teachers need time outside of the mandated teaching day for staff development, program planning, student evaluation, and so on.

From my perspective as a middle-school principal, it seems to me that issues raised by the case go beyond the experience of a single school to involve questions of policy. State departments of education must review time requirements for instructional time that they mandate to local school districts. The official definition of instructional time that "counts" in meeting state mandates may have to be broadened to include such experiences as at-home study, projects, service programs, organized athletics, and other learning experiences that take place outside of school. In fact, a new depth of community and corporate involvement may also be necessary to broaden the arena of educational opportunities for students.

The more I think about it, the more it seems that our current definition of the length of the school day for both students and staff should be reevaluated. We should look at teachers' time needs and students' time needs separately to see where that takes us. Currently, teachers spend about as much official time at school as do students. Does this make sense? Do both groups need more time? More of what kinds of time? One thing seems clear: Any effort to restructure time will surely require the support of federal, state, and local educational agencies, as well as the support of teacher associations.

Analysis: Editor

This case is a cautionary tale: Beware the results when cutting-edge practice becomes mandated orthodoxy. Here is a school that was a charter school before there were charter schools, a site-based management school before SBM was a buzzword, a school that knew what waivers it needed to create its vision of excellent education. Most important, it had control over its time and resources. Now, these types of innovations have been blessed as official policy in this district and many other places. The problem is that when abrupt expansion via policy occurs, rigidities creep in because the system itself has not been "recultured" to replace control and compliance with trust and results.

One of the more interesting passages in this case is the following:

> Our professional time was under no less pressure than it would have been in a traditional school. Yet teachers found that when control of time was in their own hands, and when staff and students were able to make so many of their own choices . . . there was much less resistance to change.

In the course of our work, we visit many schools for many purposes. We know from personal observations that these statements ring true. In schools where teachers do not feel controlled or manipulated by micromanagement of what they need to do and when they need to do it, the educational climate is more positive, less stressful, and very productive for everyone. (This is not an advertisement for completely unstructured education. Truly self-governing institutions tend to peg their standards high and set responsible limits for what is acceptable.)

This case also raises an issue about duration of time in an educational reform context. The school in question has a substantial history, and the author has institutional memory that goes back to the "good old days" of the school's formative years. Time is not going to stand still. The context and the options are going to change, but there is always a cutting edge. The challenge for this school, with its current faculty and constituency, is to decide whether it wants to continue to lead the way and then find the path that allows it to do so.

THE EROSION OF SITE-BASED, SHARED DECISION MAKING

School Profile: Monroe High School

Monroe High School is a well-established alternative high school in a small midwestern city. The school has been recovering dropouts and near-dropouts for over 20 years. It has grown from a storefront-type operation involving 3 teachers and 40 students to a campus with 34 teachers, 10 para-professionals, and more than 600 students in grades 9–12. The proportion of minority students served is slightly higher than in other district schools. The proportion of students eligible for free or reduced-price lunch is estimated to be about 70%; for the district overall, the proportion is 25%.

Monroe successfully serves a very educationally needy student population. Nearly 40% of female students are pregnant or parenting. Almost a quarter of the students live independently of their families. Upwards of 60% are adjudicated youth or in need of social services and other support. In a follow-up of one recent class a year after graduation, the principal found that 81% were employed, continuing their education, or in the armed services.

As is the case with many alternative high schools, Monroe enjoys a great deal of autonomy. This has both negative and positive aspects. For example, the school district is supportive of the school's mission but often forgets that there are five high schools, not four, when the resources are distributed. On the other hand, being largely out of sight and out of mind has allowed the faculty and administrators to develop a learner-centered program with several unique features that affect both students and teachers.

Students attend Monroe in either a morning or an afternoon session 4 days per week. This schedule is designed to accommodate other pressing responsibilities of the population served such as work, parenting, and court-required counseling. The curriculum is both interdisciplinary and competency-based. Some of the courses are called "vocademics" and combine vocational and entrepreneurial training and experience with academic content.

By design, teachers at Monroe wear a number of hats, and do so enthusiastically. In addition to their instructional duties, they develop curriculum, act as student advisors and advocates, and pursue a continuous-improvement process rooted in a good deal of discussion and debate. Their ability to focus on noninstructional aspects of their jobs is greatly facilitated by "studentless" Fridays. Teachers report that membership in the Coalition of Essential Schools and the National Education Association's Mastery Learning Project has both broadened and deepened their commitment to examining what they do and how they could do it better.

Case: High School Teacher

My school was founded in 1974 by three teachers and an administrator with a dream: to give high school dropouts a chance to continue their education in a relaxed and personal environment—an alternative school. The new school, the founders thought, should provide the personalized attention that disaffected students want and need to overcome their learning and personal problems. The school should also be a democratically run community in which teachers can apply their skills to the practice of their educational philosophies. Despite its great benefits, democratic self-governance—or site-based, shared decision making, as it is called today—has proven to be a challenge, a time-consuming process that has been difficult to sustain.

In the first years, when our school was quite small, the principal was off-site, and teachers made all decisions about students, curriculum, and the school's day-to-day operations. Flexible time was an important factor in how we did our work, and it was reflected in the daily and weekly schedules we designed. Because students attended either morning or afternoon classes, 4 days a week, we were able to reserve Fridays for teachers to participate in a staff meeting that addressed student issues, to visit students' homes, and to work collaboratively in designing and planning courses and school activities. Impromptu meetings often occurred during the week so that teachers could deal jointly with students' problems, debate curricular issues, make budget decisions, and address other school policy issues as they arose. Many spirited discussions took place around creative and sometimes wild ideas.

The 45-student "storefront" school quickly grew, but teachers continued to run the school and to maintain its student-centered approach. By its fifth year, the school had grown into two school sites, and a "lead teacher" coordinated the work of 15 teachers and 250 students at each site. Knowledge of the school's success began to spread and helped to increase the student and teacher populations, until we had to create a student waiting list. At about that time, declining enrollment in the district precipitated the closing of an elementary school. This turn of events presented an opportunity for our alternative school to combine its two storefront sites and to move into the vacant school building.

The faculty of both sites discussed and debated the merits and problems of becoming one large school. Most of us had previously taught in larger, traditional settings. We knew firsthand the isolation one feels in large schools, and we had grown to appreciate and expect a more personal approach to teaching and learning at our smaller, alternative school. For years we had made the critical decisions about how to deal with students, organize curriculum, and run our school. We even selected new teachers through a faculty interview committee. Would a larger setting and a larger faculty jeopardize our shared decision making, we wondered? We spent nearly a year—collectively and as individual school faculties—weighing the pros and cons of a merger.

With high hopes and many trepidations we merged and became a school of 26 teachers and 450 students. Our principal continued to be off-site, and the faculty continued to be responsible for school governance. We had a lead teacher to guide us, and we continued to fully debate issues and make decisions through sometimes lengthy discussions. But two changes occurred with the merger. The first was obvious: The number of teachers involved in discussions and decision making at weekly staff meetings doubled. A second, more subtle change was in the nature of our discussions and decision-making processes. Our lead teacher—and soon to be principal—chaired faculty meetings and led our discussions. Gradually, it seemed to many of us that our joint decisions were allowed to stand only if our lead teacher agreed with them. When she disagreed with a faculty decision, she would see to it that we revisited the decision at our next meeting. To many, it appeared that we were asked either to renegotiate our decisions to meet the lead teacher's preference or to "rubber-stamp" a decision that she had already made. We sensed that our lead teacher was unwilling to share authority with the faculty.

In 1984, we focused our attention and faculty discussions on becoming affiliated with the Coalition of Essential Schools. This high school reform movement, which is headed by Theodore Sizer at Brown University, is based on nine principles that grew out of a study of high schools. The principles call for schools to, among other things, personalize teaching and create an atmosphere of trust and respect for school, faculty, students, and parents.

The Coalition was looking for schools willing to embark on education reform by operationalizing the movement's nine principles. Believing that our
school already emulated the Coalition's philosophy, we decided after many
hours of debate to become an associate member of the Coalition.

The Coalition discussions were healthy and a diversion from other problems. But as some of us became more involved with the Coalition, we returned to two steadily growing problems at home: (1) the erosion of site-
based decision making at our school and (2) a lack of time to fully debate
issues and to expand our professional duties to include such things as team
teaching, crisis intervention, student counseling, and the development of new
curricula and assessments. We saw that we had a distance to travel before
we represented and modeled the Coalition's nine principles.

By then, our faculty meetings had degenerated into 2 hours of announce-
ments and general housekeeping. The in-depth discussions we used to have—
about curriculum, students' needs, the philosophical direction of the school,
and involvement with the Coalition—had ceased. Faculty members began
asking each other what had happened to our shared decision making
regarding student discipline and the school budget (a long-standing budget
committee had disappeared). Only a few teachers continued to participate
actively in full faculty meetings. Several factors probably account for this
waning participation, including the large size of the faculty, lack of understanding about shared decision making (some new teachers had come on
board without proper induction), and other interpersonal issues. Many began
to question the strong role that several individuals had in influencing faculty
decisions, given the ideal image of collaborative decision making that was
conveyed to visitors and district administrators.

Although the more autocratic approach to school governance was a more
expedient way of dealing with delicate issues at our school, it curtailed discussion and controversy among faculty. As a result, we had more time on
Fridays to make home visits, work with student advisees, and deal with other
school-related issues; but the time also seemed to be spent on more trivial
matters, such as the scheduling of special events. Many of us felt cut out of
the decision-making process that we had cherished and believed to be important. But we found that our perceptions did not match those of our lead
teacher.

Once the district administration named the lead teacher to be principal
of our school, several of us decided to voice our concerns. We were surprised to learn our principal's view of her leadership style and responsibilities. First, she perceives her style to be similar to that of the previous principal. The previous principal, she said, also directed faculty to arrive at
decisions that he wanted; he was simply better at doing that. Second, our
principal said that she sometimes becomes weary of the lengthy and some-

times heated group discussions needed to achieve consensus and that her approach can and does save time for all of us; she takes control so that we will have more time to spend on other concerns. Third, she said that, ultimately, the principal is responsible for the consequences of faculty decisions. As the principal, she is accountable to central administration, to parents, and to others. If we make a bad decision, we leave her accountable. We understood these views, but they did not address our problem.

My frustration led me back to school—to continue my education and to simply move on with my life. Once there, however, the study of educational renewal intrigued me. Coursework in organizational change, educational leadership, and the micropolitics of schools gave me insight into the dynamics at work in my own school and others, particularly the relationships between teachers and principals. The writings of prominent researchers helped me understand the concept of school culture and the power that culture exerts within a high school setting.

As we have continued to struggle with change in our school—change associated with our membership in the Coalition and with other concerns regarding how best to serve our students—time remains a central issue. How can we change the structure of our school day and improve the design of our schedule? How can we expand our services for students within the same time constraints? I have discovered that the more I learn from my own research and reading, the more I question myself and others. If site-based decision making is to be effective, what should we do differently, and what are reasonable expectations for the process itself and the outcomes? What are the faculty members' individual and group responsibilities? How do we secure time to discuss, debate, and redesign a new model of site-based decision making that we can sustain? Ultimately, what must we give up in order to gain from shared decision making, not only for ourselves but for each other and our students?

Commentary: University Dean

Site-based, shared decision making is an ideal concept implemented by imperfect human beings. No matter how noble the intentions and how great the abilities of those involved, simple human frailties cause these processes to vary in quality over time. Relatively smoothly operating eras are inevitably followed by more messy, conflict-filled periods (and, one hopes, vice versa). The frailties that most often draw attention are those of the principal. Even when other variables—such as a sudden increase in school size or a dramatic drop in funding—complicate matters, we tend to focus on the principal when things are not going well. The principal almost always draws the heat of people's frustrations.

In the case described here, when precious time dedicated to critical teaching and learning issues has somehow slipped away, the principal emerges as the culprit. Even though the principal, as I can personally testify, has enormous ability and compassion, she appears here as the primary cause of the "erosion." And perhaps she is, but I do not think so. Instead, I believe that the case illustrates the inadequacies of the principalship for meeting the needs of the site-based school. The principalship fosters, much like the college deanship, dependency and centralization of power, rather than distribution of authority throughout the school. Unless specific structures are in place to protect shared authority, authority will gravitate to the principal. Inevitably, the principal's priorities are disproportionally weighted in school business; it is the natural progression.

This case is particularly interesting because the school under examination did not have an on-site principal for years. Instead, three lead teachers shared formal on-site leadership responsibilities, while the principal of another building—who could not possibly interfere too much—was the nominal, final authority for the school's business. This arrangement worked well for a long time, but eventually the district's administration preferred to have an on-site principal and elevated a lead teacher to the principalship.

Bingo! At that point, nothing short of heroic measures could have prevented almost any principal's concern for efficiency from transforming the existing order. But what sort of heroic steps might have been taken? It is easier to pose the question than to answer it. I believe that site-based, shared-decision-making schools would best be served by a leadership structure like that of an unprogrammed Quaker meeting. Such an approach would call for a chosen leader, corresponding to the Quakers' "clerk" of the meeting, to facilitate school meetings and officially represent the school to the outside world for a limited term. During this time, major tasks would be delegated to a set of standing committees, all of which would vigilantly practice consensus decision making before presenting their recommendations to the entire school faculty and staff for final consensus decisions.

However, this sort of radical shift is not likely to be widely embraced. History shows that Quaker meeting governance practices have not been widely adopted, even at many Quaker schools. Because such governance practices can be very time-consuming, they may be seen as impractical, given the rapid acceleration of communications and decision making in our postmodern world. So, might some more palatable compromise approach be developed?

I am not sure, but at my college we are now experimenting with a 20-member coordinating council convened by the dean and consisting of a broad cross-section of division chairs, faculty, staff, and students. The purpose of the council is to wrestle with big issues, engage in strategic planning, and set the agenda for monthly, college-wide meetings. The 20 people on the coordinating council are now dealing with matters over which the dean used to have virtually sole discretion. The coordinating council serves as a check on the dean's power.

Our preliminary experience with this new governance structure is encouraging, but it is too early to judge its overall success. Still, site-based management schools might take notice and consider their own local variations. Although it is unlikely to keep a real autocratic principal in line, a governance council such as ours might serve to keep shared decision-making efforts on course. Consequently, faculty and staff agreement over the use of valuable time might be better preserved.

Commentary: Principal

Originally, the alternative high school examined in this case was composed of a small group of dedicated teachers working with students whom no one else wanted to serve. Left alone to fend for themselves, the teachers, it seems, interpreted this arrangement to be site-based management. The school's "invisibility," I suspect, gave students and teachers alike a sense of autonomy that seemed like site-based management. In fact, the alternative school was never officially conferred the authority to govern itself; it was simply ignored by the establishment. Thanks to the school's dedicated and self-directed staff, the district received state funding for the alternative school's many high-need students without any of the headaches. The school was out of sight and out of mind—a perfect solution from the district's perspective at the time.

A subsequent decision to join the two "storefront" operations and move them to an abandoned elementary school building meant that the alternative school's invisibility was no longer possible. The school would now be noticed, and once noticed, it had to be accountable to a central authority: an on-site principal who would answer to the district office. Additionally, by moving the alternative school into an abandoned elementary school building, the district could show that the building—a valuable community resource—was not being wasted, but was being put to good use as a more suitable facility for needy students. Make no mistake about it, the move to the elementary school building was a political decision as well as a financial one. The move transformed the alternative school into new turf that would come under the district's control.

This case argues that the main point of contention at the alternative school is which management theory is most appropriate: hierarchical or collaborative. Although it may appear to be so on the surface, a closer look reveals a struggle over political power and school control. Site-based, shared decision making is not simply a matter of teachers' being free to do what they want to do when they want to do it. It is much more than that. Like all school governance alternatives, site-based, shared decision making is at its core a bureaucratic arrangement within a political context. This case suggests that site-based decision making is wholly absent of political interest and that hierarchical management is almost solely a matter of political posturing. In fact, both hierarchical and site-based, collaborative governance are political options that eventually get down to who controls whom. The more important question is, "To what end?"

For me, the most important but unexplored dimension of this case is the outcome of school governance in terms of student welfare. The proof of a school's value and success can be determined only by measures of student accomplishment and satisfaction, not by which governance or management method is practiced. Student accomplishment must be central to any discussion of school governance. It is only in light of a thorough examination of student outcomes that one can usefully make judgments about the value of any school governance option.

Commentary: Teacher

As a fellow teacher in the school described in this case, I am especially interested in commenting on a concern about site-based, shared decision making that is attributed to the principal: that time is lost by engaging school faculty in long and potentially divisive discussions about controversial topics. My observation is that not allowing these discussions to take place—discussions about issues that teachers view as central to the school's mission and healthy operation—has resulted in two damaging consequences that have adversely affected how our school treats educational issues.

The first consequence is the negative impact on faculty cohesion. The decrease in shared decision making at our school has resulted in feelings of alienation and disengagement, and the development of factions within the faculty. Lack of faculty cohesion has resulted in the loss of additional and sometimes unique perspectives on and solutions to educational issues. Because they have little input in the decision-making process, several faculty members have decided that it is better to focus their time, energy, and talents on other things. Internal divisions have resulted in certain factions' spending an inordinate amount of unscheduled time complaining about other faculty members' class loads and contributions to the school. In addition, time is spent protecting "turf," rather than working for the collective benefit of the entire school. These activities not only represent a substantial amount of lost time; they are by their nature counterproductive to the work of the school.

The second consequence of the erosion of shared decision making in our school is the loss of a common vision among faculty members. An attempt to define our school's culture was curtailed when the discussion touched on sensitive areas, such as the decline in communication and increase in factions among the staff. Efforts to delineate the skills, abilities, and attitudes we want our graduates to possess have been tabled because of the time necessary to reach consensus. It is my belief that if we had devoted sufficient time to addressing these issues, we could make subsequent decisions more efficiently and more effectively. A clearly articulated, shared vision is essential to the school's work, and it is something that must be constantly recreated through faculty deliberations. Common vision is the conceptual framework that gives faculty discussion meaning and focus about all issues. Without it, we spend time on unproductive conversation and activities that distract us from our most important work. We are spending a lot of time on school concerns in any case. It would make more sense for that time to be put to productive use through collaborative decision making.

Analysis: Editor

This case illustrates the robustness of what Yale professor Seymour Sarason (1971) long ago dubbed the "regularities" of schooling—that is, the structures and relationships that have defined life in schools for a century and are so resistant to change. When the alternative programs were storefronts, they did not seem like schools. Therefore, different structures and relationships were eminently possible. According to this case, as soon as the programs were joined into a larger unit and housed in a real school building, many of the regularities resiliently bounced right back. Why did this occur, and what might be done to restore shared decision making and a more cohesive faculty culture?

Our outsider view of this school is somewhat different from that of the case writer. We selected it as a site for our study of time and student learning because of its adaptation of academic time to meet the needs of a unique student population. By all the evidence, it produces successful student outcomes through a schedule involving less daily and weekly time in school but a longer duration of time to high school graduation. When we visited, we were also impressed with the faculty's innovative approaches to curriculum and instruction and the substantiveness of the extended faculty meeting on the day when students do not attend school.

Perhaps the problem here is one of space rather than time. As the school has gotten larger (although it remains considerably smaller than the typical urban or suburban comprehensive high school), the feelings of intimacy and cohesiveness among the total faculty have no doubt been reduced. Loss of this culture would naturally be felt most strongly by the pioneers of the alternative program, such as the case writer. However, others apparently are seeking heightened camaraderie and intimacy as well—a natural tendency in an institutional setting. The problem is that the collegial groups have become dysfunctional factions, arguing over process issues. One solution might be to restructure the school around self-directed teams of teachers and students with decision-making authority over and accountability for the substance, direction, and results of the core technologies of education: curriculum and instruction.

CHAPTER 5

In Conclusion: New Ways to Think About Teachers and Time

Andy Hargreaves

The stories in this casebook make one thing very clear: If there is a single thing that teachers always need more of, it is time. There just never seems to be enough of it. Getting through the content, hearing all your students read, writing up reports, keeping up to date with marking papers, phoning all those parents, squeezing in planning meetings with colleagues, learning new computer skills, trying out a new teaching strategy, cooking a proper supper once you get home—there do not seem to be enough hours in the day to get through all these things.

Time is a chronic problem in almost all kinds of teaching. It comes with the territory. This is because of the nature of teaching itself as an endless job that is never finished, never over, never done. Teachers cannot sew up their patients or close their cases. In teaching, you can always spend more time on a child's problem, write more detailed and supportive comments on students' work, improve the quality of display in the classroom, or prepare more interesting activities for the next unit of work. Teaching is a caring profession. In an endless job, this means that teachers can never quite care enough. Teachers are therefore always haunted by feelings of guilt and inadequacy (Hargreaves, 1994). At its best, the guilt that comes from endless aspiration is a spur to dedicated professionalism. At its worst, it can turn altruistic enthusiasts into self-denying martyrs and cheerless workaholics.

The fashionable quest for schools and teachers to pursue continuous improvement (Rosenholtz, 1989) can unintendedly intensify these time pressures and add to teachers' guilt burdens. The line between continuous improvement and interminable improvement is a fine one, and school change efforts often fall foul of it (Hargreaves, 1995a). Indeed, educational change and school reform initiatives can quickly turn the chronic condition of teachers' time into an acute one of crisis proportions. Change is not always good. And endless change may be not only unsettling, but positively destructive (Giddens, 1995).

Time has long been recognized as a serious obstacle to successful school change (Fullan, 1991). Teachers' existing responsibilities of classroom preparation, teaching, and grading make it hard for them to find time to falter through the first steps of new classroom teaching strategies; to observe and talk to other teachers who have learned to practice these strategies successfully; to plan the many tasks required for even just one lesson of cooperative learning; to undertake an authentic assessment with one classroom group while being assured that all other students are engaged in something productive too; to write sensitive anecdotal report card comments, where a precoded computerized statement used to suffice; or to meet with colleagues to rewrite the curriculum so that it will fit newly mandated common learning outcomes.

If the time crunches that teachers experience are not properly dealt with, someone or something eventually suffers. This might be the educational change initiative that exacerbated the time problems in the first place. Teachers may protect their time by ignoring the innovation, slowing down its implementation, selecting only those bits that can be integrated easily into their current practice, or creatively redefining it so it justifies what they have already been doing (Werner, 1988).

If the change does not suffer from teachers' time pressures, the students might, as teachers are deflected from their classroom priorities. Ingvarson, Chadbourne, and Culton (1994) relate how Australian teachers who have been recognized as "advanced skills teachers" find themselves "living off past preparation" with their own classes, so they can make time for the new administrative and leadership responsibilities they are expected to carry out. Richardson, Casanova, Placier, and Guilfoyle (1989) found that in a school reform effort that was designed to benefit students "at-risk," the classes from which teachers were most often pulled to participate in staff development and team leadership activities connected to the change were the very classes of the most needy at-risk students (with the most expendable schedules) whom the reforms were meant to benefit. Neufeld (1991) found equally perverse processes at work in an elementary school he researched that was implementing active learning: The time demands of coping with the initiative and its group-based performance assessments were so great that teachers no longer had time to care for their students more informally during less structured and scheduled moments in the school day.

A third cost exacted by the time crunches of teaching is on teachers themselves. Teachers may become overwhelmed by the increasing demands of reform, and may become crippled by "conscientiousness" as they attempt to implement the reforms faithfully in ways that will benefit their students (Campbell & Neill, 1994). Burnout follows swiftly on such unsustainable dedication. Or cynicism creeps in if the changes to which teachers have committed themselves are then capriciously discarded in favor of purportedly new or better ones (Huberman, 1994).

Clearly, time is more than a trivial problem for teachers. Shortage of time warps the course of innovation. It draws teachers away from their students. And it drains the energy of teachers themselves. The problem is not getting any better. Many researchers have remarked that the work of teachers is becoming more and more intensified as teachers' responsibilities widen, the pace of change increases, reform initiatives are heaped chaotically on one another, and self-management diverts teachers from the classroom to attend to growing burdens of administration and committee work that used to be managed elsewhere (Apple, 1989; Densmore, 1987; Hargreaves, 1994; Robertson, 1993).

The evidence seems to be accumulating, then, that the role of teacher is expanding and becoming more complex, while the time to accomplish teachers' work generally remains fixed. Teachers' unions are inclined to argue that relief is to be found in more teachers and smaller classes—but this would not deal with all the other demands from outside of the classroom that teachers are having to address. More preparation time away from class is also a commonly advocated solution, but my own research has shown that, beyond a certain point, many elementary teachers have reservations about spending substantial time away from their own classrooms (Hargreaves, 1994). Getting more time is no good if it takes teachers away from what they think is most important. Teachers often also wish that school reform could be slowed down, or put on hold. But while too much educational reform is definitely faddish, hurried, and ill-thought-out, the rapid pace of technological, economic, and sociocultural change means that schools cannot be frozen in time while past innovations are institutionalized and consolidated. The world will not wait until teachers decide to catch up.

So what other options are there? How should teachers, administrators, and policymakers tackle the time problem in teaching? Three broad approaches have been commonly suggested. The first of these sees teachers and schools as prisoners of time. This approach heightens our awareness that the time structures of teaching and schooling are historically arbitrary and can be changed. A second approach treats teachers and schools as time bandits that can capture time and use it for their own purposes. Third are approaches that recognize that time is subjective, that we hold different conceptions of it, and that only by being partners in time can we come to develop shared understandings of the impact of time on our work, and shared agreements about the ways in which such time might best be restructured.

PRISONERS OF TIME

In a historical study of U.S. education reform efforts, Tyack and Tobin (1994) argue that schooling is in some respects like a language. It has a fundamental grammar. Just as the grammar of language frames how we can speak, the grammar of schooling frames how we can educate. Each grammar has its special origins. But once established, each grammar also becomes highly stable, slow to change. Tyack and Tobin support their claims through investigating five educational reforms. Two of these—the graded school (which processes its students in age-graded cohorts through standardized curricula) and Carnegie units or course credits (which constitute the criteria for high school graduation and university entrance)—became institutionalized decades ago and now make up the contemporary grammar of schooling. Three other educational changes—the Dalton Plan, the Eight Year Reform, and Flexible High Schools—enjoyed only temporary or localized success because they contravened the grammar of schooling. The fact that most of you do not recognize them proves the point. In a way, they were nonstandard, localized dialects of change, used only for a short time or on the margins of educational life.

Particular distributions and organizations of time are basic to the given grammar of schooling. As the National Commission on Time and Learning (1994) has put it:

> Learning in [our schools] is a prisoner of time. For the past 150 years . . . [public] schools have held time constant and let learning vary. . . . Our schools and the people involved with them . . . are captives of clock and calendars. The boundaries of student growth are defined by schedules, bells, buses and vacations instead of standards for students and learning. (p. 7)

Handed down, taken-for-granted time structures in schooling just do not seem appropriate anymore for the kinds of learning students need to do and the kinds of challenges teachers face. For example, at present, "a school does not have much flexibility for structuring into the schedule the kind of time that teachers need to make school a collegial effort" (Donahoe, 1993, p. 299). Understanding that existing time structures for schooling are not themselves timeless, recognizing that they are not the only possible structures there can be, can help us begin to deconstruct our assumptions about time and discover how it affects the possibilities for change and improvement in teaching. It can help us move beyond squeezing new goals for learning into the time structures we are burdened with, to addressing the needs and purposes of learning first, then working out how we can organize and structure school time to meet them. Most school structures are anachronisms in relation to our current educational purposes. Understanding this is the first principle from which to build more creative and supportive approaches to reorganizing time in teachers' work.

TIME BANDITS

Once we have broken free conceptually from being prisoners of time, many people believe that we can then commandeer time for our own purposes. Numerous possibilities have been proposed and experimented with in this regard. Some of the key questions that we should be asking include the following:

- Why remain wedded to a traditional school day that starts at 9:00 A.M. and ends at 4:00 P.M.? Very hot climatic conditions in some regions of the country and parts of the world make it almost impossible for students to concentrate and learn in the middle of the day. While teachers and students in this country go through the motions of learning during the hottest time of the day, their Mediterranean counterparts start and finish much earlier to make best use of the available climatic conditions for learning. Alternatively, why should learning end at 4 P.M., for students, for adults, or for the community? All-day schooling carries financial benefits and potential benefits for community learning as well.
- Why retain a school year that is geared to the rhythm of the agricultural seasons when year-round schooling might be educationally sound and make economic sense? Are lengthy vacations good for learning when considerable time for review work is required at the begining of every school year? Does the rhythm of the agricultural seasons work as well for teachers in the darkening days of winter, when they have been toiling for weeks on end, with no letup? In school districts where school overcrowding has forced a change to year-round schedules, teachers and families have frequently become advocates of patterns such as 45 days of school followed by 15 days of vacation.
- Why not restructure the school day to provide teachers with more time for preparation, professional learning, and collaborative planning with colleagues within school hours? Darling-Hammond (1994a) notes that compared with other activities, "no other nation requires teachers to teach more hours per week than the U.S." (p. 16). However, by adding just 15 minutes to each instructional day, children can be sent home early on every tenth day to create 105 minutes of in-school time for team planning and other work with colleagues (Lieberman, 1995). The current scarcity of time for these purposes results from a system that, compared with other countries,

invests less in its front-line workers, and more in bureaucratic systems for supervising them. These bureaucratic priorities should not be immune from restructuring.

• Why not reconfigure secondary school schedules (e.g., along the principles of block scheduling or core grouping) to reduce the number of students teachers must see each week and to increase the time available for them to implement new, more complex teaching strategies? Theodore Sizer (1992) and the Coalition for Essential Schools have argued that no teacher should see more than 80 students a week. My own research has found that even secondary school teachers who are highly skilled in and committed to new teaching strategies like cooperative learning complain that implementation of reforms within conventional secondary school timetables is exhausting because, as a teacher, you are always "on," having to stagger from one bell-bound interactive performance to the next (Hargreaves, Leithwood, Gerin-Lajoie, Cousin, & Thiessen, 1993). Core blocking (sometimes referred to as houses, families, or pods) assigns four or five teachers to 100 or so students. This strategy can circumvent many problems by (1) giving teachers more time/flexibility to use complex classroom strategies; (2) enabling one teacher to work with a small group while another handles the rest of the class; (3) reducing the number of students teachers have to get to know so they can assess, report on, and care and plan for their students more effectively; (4) creating a functioning community of students, which tends to reduce disciplinary problems and distractions; and (5) establishing a coherent community of colleagues who will find it easier to coordinate their efforts with core blocking than through conventional, fragmented schedules that are more typical of secondary schools.

• Why not create flexible timetables and schedules in order to accommodate periodic changes and adjustments that are likely to benefit both teachers and students? Timetables or schedules can be suspended for a day, a week, or more to bring students and colleagues together to work on issues of immediate interest or on integrated themes that cut across conventional subject boundaries. A curriculum based on learning outcomes can release teachers from their fear of failing to cover the required content that otherwise often accompanies innovative efforts. Suspensions of existing structures can allow teachers and schools to experiment with reconfigurations of time and space in ways that benefit their students and themselves, through special projects, cross-grade groupings, peer tutoring, and the like.

• Why not tap into other resources (e.g., student teachers, adults in the community, technology) to lighten the load of the classroom work and create more time flexibility in teachers' workdays? Student teachers can be clustered together in professional development schools, integrating their own efforts with experienced teachers' professional development, and providing human resources as these schools pursue collective improvement (Darling-Hammond, 1994b). Adults other than licensed teachers can be brought into the school to work alongside teachers in various support roles (Epstein, 1988). Resources can be reallocated from supervising bureaucracies to school-level supports for teachers (Fenstermacher, 1990). The work of teaching might even be restructured to include the kind of technical assistance that is available in other professions such as dental hygienists, nurse practitioners, and paralegals—where teacher support personnel would not merely cut up paper and photocopy worksheets, but also take on some of the simpler tasks of instruction itself (Hargreaves, 1995b). In some places, this happens already; in others, policies prohibit paraprofessionals from directly instructing children. Students can also provide support for teachers in the form of peer-assisted learning, gaining valuable leadership experience in the process. Similarly, technology can relieve teachers from some of their time burdens by engaging students periodically with carefully structured programs of self-monitored learning.

Time is not a fixed quantity. We can capture it and manipulate it for our own purposes. Less preciousness and self-protectiveness about our own professional status and about our sense of indispensability as educators might also enable us to draw on other technical and human resources to ease the time burdens of teaching. But it is not as if the sorts of provisions I have described are unfamiliar to teachers and those who control the conditions of their work. The problem does not seem to be one of imagining alternative structures of time. It is more a question of feeling able to implement these new structures successfully. This problem of implementation takes us beyond the question of how time can be redesigned by administration to how time is experienced by teachers themselves.

PARTNERS IN TIME

Why does it seem to be so hard to restructure teachers' time? Why is it so difficult to work smarter instead of harder? One reason is that sometimes the expectations and the points of comparison with time structures elsewhere are unrealistic. For instance, Barlow and Robertson (1994) take issue with common comparisons between a 185-day U.S. school year and a 243-day Japanese one, noting that the figure of 243 days is simply "the allowable maximum days Japanese schools are permitted to be open. . . . No school, however, comes close to this number of teaching days" (p. 34). Moreover, they say, the official number of Japanese school days includes many non-instructional days for sports and celebrations. In other words, crude quantitative, "objective" comparisons of time allocations between different countries in terms of school year, school days, and so forth should not be taken at face value. These figures usually mask all kinds of subjective subtleties and complexities of time use within them.

Second, increasing the number of instructional days (or hours) does not necessarily lead to better instruction. More time does not always mean more learning. It depends on what the time is used for. The activities and purposes of teaching and learning, not just the sheer quantity of it, have to be addressed in any effort to increase school time. If children are failing at something the school is doing, simply exposing them to more of it is not going to solve the problem.

Third, some attempts to solve the time problem in school inadvertently add to it. One principal recently proposed to me that school lunch hours could be used more productively as a time to bring teachers together—yet this overlooks the value such seemingly "slack time" can have for helping teachers relax and replenish themselves, or for enabling them to organize materials and otherwise prepare for their own classes. Similarly, self-managing schools appear to be eating up much of the slack time among teachers by downloading onto them additional responsibilities that used to be handled by the system. Slack time may not be "slack" or "spare" at all. Just because it is not scheduled for meetings or other formal business does not mean that it is not subjectively valuable to teachers. Intruding on it may seriously damage the quality of work teachers are able to do.

Fourth, reassignments of time that seem perfectly rational to teachers in schools can strike others as deeply threatening and problematic. If schools announce early closings on every tenth day for staff development purposes, bus companies may resist all efforts to tamper with the school bus schedule. Some parents will worry if restructuring of school time challenges their own images of "real school" (Metz, 1991)—the kind of school they believe worked for them and that they feel will ensure success for their own children. Other families with two working parents will be concerned about child care. Unions may also be suspicious of proposals to restructure time, seeing them (sometimes correctly) as thinly veiled moves toward heightened teacher exploitation.

What all these problems indicate is that restructuring teacher time is no simple matter. How time is structured and organized means different things to different people. People experience time differently. Its subjective meaning varies among them. A restructuring of time that seems to make eminent sense to administrators may be deeply problematic to parents, union representatives, and classroom teachers themselves. Since it is teachers who must live with the implications of restructured school time, it is extremely important that we find ways to evoke and elicit their experiences of time and its restructuring, and that we include these experiences and understandings in any attempts to restructure school time more meaningfully for the educational challenges of today. We need to explore how teachers can move beyond being prisoners of time, to become partners in time with others who are involved in positive educational change. The purpose of this book is to stimulate this kind of exploration.

REFLECTING ON THE CASES

As explained in the Introduction, the editors of this book wanted to create a process and a product where teachers' own voices could speak openly and directly about their experiences of time and change in their work. Our purpose was to present some cases or capsules of time that teachers wrote themselves and that might stimulate recognition and reflection among teachers and other educators elsewhere. Most important, we did not want the process and the teachers who participated in it to suffer from the very problems we were asking them to address. We did not want to gather interview data from weary teachers, in hurried moments, snatched from their school day. We wanted, rather, to make available a time and a space in which teachers could reflect together more deeply on their experiences of their work and their workplaces—and do that without fear of other colleagues or children bursting in, or guilt about pressing obligations that such a seeming indulgence might be jeopardizing.

It has been immensely exciting to witness the process that led to the teachers' self-authored narratives included in Chapters 2 to 4. The capsules of time that they created are candid, constructive, and critical. As documents of teachers' own subjective experiences of time in an educational world of accelerating change, the cases should make riveting reading for fellow teachers, who will identify and empathize with these thoughtful reflections on front-line teaching. For administrators and policymakers, the cases should make salutary reading of smelling-salt proportions! Few will escape twinges of conscience as bold administrative visions of reform and restructuring are seen to be overambitious, insensitive to teachers' own time frames, or insufficiently inclusive of teachers' own input. What is clear from these case descriptions and the commentaries on them is that teachers do not have a single, unified perspective on time and educational change. What educational change has meant for teacher time is sometimes contested between case writers and commentators, often in the same case account.

The beauty of these time capsules, therefore, is that they do not come to elegant closure. Such intellectual closure is achieved only in the aesthetic schemes of academic writing, where knowledge as certainty receives high professional rewards. Rich, vivid, and evocative as they are, the cases show variation, disagreement, and even uncertainty in teachers' experiences of time, as an object of educational change and also as an obstacle to it. This openness of the texts makes them all the better for other educators to reflect on and interact with, empowering them to draw on and develop their own texts and narratives of experience as they work with colleagues to understand the importance of time in their work and address how, together, they might best restructure it.

Many teachers and schools, I have argued, work within time warps—within temporal grammars of schooling that are suited for other purposes in other times. Perversely, it is also the case that time warps our efforts to undertake productive educational change, including change in the time structures of schooling itself. Time is not just something we can count, calculate, manage, and manipulate. It is something that is deeply embedded in the subjective life and work of those who experience it. We can only really understand and address the place of time in educational change by directly engaging with its personal meaning. It is good that existing structures of school time are no longer sacrosanct and that policymakers are starting to address them as an issue. But, given the deeply subjective and embedded nature of time in teachers' work, it is vital that teachers' voices have some say in school-level, district-level, and state-level discussions and decisions about how time in teaching might be restructured. We hope that the perceptions about time and change that teachers and other educators have presented in this book will contribute to those discussions and deepen the dialogue about this exceedingly important aspect of school reform.

References

Adelman, N. E., Haslam, M. B., & Pringle, B.A. (1996). *The uses of time for teaching and learning. Volume I: Findings and conclusions.* Washington, DC: U.S. Department of Education, Office of Educational Research and Improvement.

Apple, M. (1989). *Teachers and texts.* New York: Routledge.

Barlow, M., & Robertson, J. (1994). *Class warfare: The assault on Canada's schools.* Toronto: Key Porter Books.

Barth, R. (1990). *Improving schools from within.* San Francisco: Jossey-Bass.

Campbell, R. J., & Neill, S. R. (1994). *Primary teachers at work.* London: Routledge.

Carnegie Council on Adolescent Development. (1989). *Turning points: Preparing American youth for the 21st century.* Washington, DC: Author.

Darling-Hammond, L. (1994a, November). *The current status of teaching and teacher development in the United States.* Unpublished background paper prepared for the National Commission on Teaching and America's Future, Teachers College, New York.

Darling-Hammond, L. (Ed.). (1994b). *Professional development schools.* New York: Teachers College Press.

Densmore, K. (1987). Professionalism, proletarization and teachers' work. In T. Popkewitz (Ed.), *Critical studies in teacher education* (pp. 130–160). London: Falmer Press.

Donahoe, T. (1993, December). Finding the way: Structure, time and culture in school improvement. *Phi Delta Kappan,* pp. 298–305.

Epstein, J. (1988). *Schools in the center: Schools, family, peers, and community. Connections for more effective middle grade schools and students.* Baltimore: Johns Hopkins University Center for Research on Elementary and Middle Schools.

Fenstermacher, G. D. (1990). Some moral considerations on teaching as a profession. In J. Goodlad, R. Soder, & K. Sirotnik (Eds.), *The moral dimension of teaching* (pp. 13–15). San Francisco: Jossey-Bass.

Fullan, M. (1991). *The new meaning of educational change.* New York: Teachers College Press.

Fullan, M. (1993). *Change forces.* London: Falmer Press.

Giddens, A. (1995). *Beyond left and right.* Stanford, CA: Stanford University Press.

Hargreaves, A. (1991). Teaching and guilt: Exploring the feelings of teaching. *Teaching and Teacher Education,* 7(5/6), 491–505.

Hargreaves, A. (1994). *Changing teachers, changing times: Teachers' work and culture in the postmodern age.* London: Cassell; New York: Teachers College Press; Toronto: OISE Press.

Hargreaves, A. (1995a). Renewal in the Age of Paradox. *Education Leadership, 52*(7), 14–19.

Hargreaves, A. (1995b, July). *Rethinking educational change.* Keynote speech presented to the International Conference of the Australian Council for Educational Administration, Sydney.

Hargreaves, A., Leithwood, K., Gerin-Lajoie, D., Cousin, B., & Thiessen, D. (1993). *Years of transition: Times for change.* Toronto: Queen's Printer.

Huberman, M. (1994). *The lives of teachers.* London: Cassell; New York: Teachers College Press.

Ingvarson, L., Chadbourne, R., & Culton, W. (1994, April). *Implementing new career structures for teachers: A study of the Advanced Skills Teachers in Australia.* Paper presented at the annual meeting of the American Education Research Association, San Francisco.

Kentucky Department of Education. (1992). *Mathematics portfolio teacher's guide.* Frankfurt: Author.

Lieberman, A. (Ed.). (1995). *The work of restructuring schools.* New York: Teachers College Press.

McAninch, A. (1993). *Teacher thinking and the case method: Theory and future directions.* New York: Teachers College Press.

Metz, M. (1991). New School: A universal drama amid desperate experience. In D. Mitchell & M. Goertz (Eds.), *Education politics for the new century: The twentieth anniversary yearbook of the Politics of Education Association* (pp. 75–91). Philadelphia: Falmer Press.

National Commission on Time and Learning. (1994). *Prisoners of time.* Washington, DC: U.S. Department of Education.

National Council of Teachers of Mathematics. (1989). *Curriculum and evaluation standards for school mathematics.* Reston, VA: Author.

Neufeld, J. (1991). Curriculum reform and the time of care. *Curriculum Journal, 2*(3), 285–300.

Richardson, V., Casanova, U., Placier, P., & Guilfoyle, K. (1989). *School children at risk.* London: Falmer Press.

Robertson, S. (1993). The politics of devolution: Self management and post-Fordism in schools. In J. Smyth (Ed.), *A socially critical view of the self-managing school* (pp. 117–136). London: Falmer Press.

Rosenholtz, S. (1989). *Teachers' workplace.* New York: Longmans.

Sarason, S. (1971). *The culture of the school and the problem of change.* Boston: Allyn & Bacon.

Sarason, S. (1990). *The predictable failure of educational reform.* San Francisco: Jossey-Bass.

Sarason, S. (1996). *Revisiting "The culture of the school and the problem of change."* New York: Teachers College Press.

Shulman, J. (Ed.). (1992). *Case methods in teacher education.* New York: Teachers College Press.

Shulman, L. (1986). Those who understand: Knowledge growth in teaching. *Educational Researcher, 15*(4), 4–14.

Shulman, L. (1987). Knowledge and teaching: Foundations of the new reform. *Harvard Educational Review, 57*(1), 1–22.

Sizer, T. (1992). *Horace's school: Redeveloping the American high school.* Boston: Houghton-Mifflin.

Tyack, D., & Tobin, W. (1994). The grammar of schooling: Why has it been so hard to change? *American Educational Research Journal, 31*(3), 453–480.

Wassermann, S. (1993). *Getting down to cases: Learning to teach with case studies.* New York: Teachers College Press.

Wassermann, S. (1994). *Introduction to case method teaching: A guide to the galaxy.* New York: Teachers College Press.

Weiss, C., Cambone, J., & Wyeth, A. (1992). Trouble in paradise: Teacher conflicts in shared decision making. *Educational Administration Quarterly, 28,* 350–367.

Werner, W. (1988). Program implementation and experienced time. *Alberta Journal of Educational Research, 34*(2), 90–108.

Index

About the Editors

Nancy E. Adelman is a Senior Research Associate in SRI International's Arlington, Virginia, office, where she specializes in research and evaluation of education reform strategies and professional development for teachers. She directed the federally funded Study of the Uses of Time for Teaching and Learning, which supported development of the teacher cases that appear in this book. She also directed a follow-up study about uses of teachers' professional time in the United States, Germany, and Japan. She holds a doctorate from Teachers College, Columbia University, and is an associate author (with Michael S. Knapp and associates) of *Teaching for Meaning in High-Poverty Classrooms*.

Karen Panton Walking Eagle is a Senior Research Associate with Policy Studies Associates in Washington, D.C., where she specializes in research and evaluation of education reform strategies, programs and policies that address the educational needs of youth at risk, and professional development. She recently directed a federally funded study of school districts' plans to address the academic and cultural needs of American Indian students and co-authored (with Leslie M. Anderson and Matthew I. Janger) *An Evaluation of State and Local Efforts to Serve the Educational Needs of Homeless Children and Youth*. She has also contributed to several evaluations of programs and initiatives designed to improve pre-service and in-service training for new and experienced teachers. She holds a master's degree in education from Harvard University and a master's degree in public administration from Columbia University's School of International and Public Affairs.

Andy Hargreaves is Director of and Professor in the International Centre for Educational Change at the Ontario Institute for Studies in Education. Before moving to North America in 1987, he taught primary school and lectured in several English universities. He is widely involved in consultation, research, and improvement activities with teachers' unions, universities, school districts, education ministries, and charitable foundations around the world, and has held visiting professorships in England, Australia, Sweden, Spain, and Japan. He is in high demand among these groups as a dynamic and motivational keynote speaker and workshop leader.

The author and editor of more than 20 books and monographs in education, he has established an international reputation as a leading authority and innovative thinker in the fields of teacher development, the culture of the school, and educational reform. His book *Changing Teachers, Changing Times* received the 1995 Outstanding Writing Award from the American Association of Colleges for Teacher Education. Among his other recent books are *Schooling for Change* (with Lorna Earl and Jim Ryan) and *Teachers' Professional Lives* (edited with Ivor Goodson). He is also the editor of the 1997 ASCD Yearbook, *Rethinking Educational Change with Heart and Mind.*

BELMONT UNIVERSITY LIBRARY

BELMONT UNIVERSITY LIBRARY

DATE DUE

GAYLORD			PRINTED IN U.S.A.